My Dear Old Thing
Talking Cricket

Henry Blofeld

STANLEY PAUL

LONDON · SYDNEY · AUCKLAND · JOHANNESBURG

Stanley Paul & Co. Ltd
An imprint of Century Hutchinson Ltd
62–65 Chandos Place, London WC2N 4NW

Century Hutchinson Australia (Pty) Ltd
89–91 Albion Street, Surry Hills NSW 2010

Century Hutchinson New Zealand Limited
PO Box 40–086, Glenfield, Auckland 10

Century Hutchinson South Africa (Pty) Ltd
PO Box 337, Bergvlei 2012, South Africa

First published 1988

Set in 10½ pt Linotron Garamond by Deltatype, Ellesmere Port
Printed and bound in Great Britain by Scotprint, Musselburgh

ISBN 0 09 173704 4

Photographic Acknowledgement: the author and publishers would like to thank Adrian Murrell/All Sport, who provided most of the photographs, and Owen Jones for permission to reproduce their copyright material.

CONTENTS

To Tony Facciolo (of Sydney's Sheraton
Wentworth Hotel) – quite simply, the
best concierge in the world who also
presides over a personal watering hole of
unusual excellence midway between
the Sydney Cricket Ground and the
Sheraton Wentworth Hotel.

Captains' Progress

West Indies in Australia 1984–85 ● two captains depart, Clive
Lloyd gloriously, Kim Hughes rather less so ● the forces ranged
against Hughes ● maladroit ACB manoeuvres ● Hughes
hooks once too much ● his tearful farewell ● was he pushed
or did he fall? ● Lloyd as captain and batsman ● fast bowlers,
over-rates and the Laws ● an ugly West Indies–New Zealand
series in retrospect.

The 1984–85 season in Australia revolved round the story of two captains
who could hardly have been more contrasting figures – Clive Lloyd and
Kim Hughes. Lloyd was on his last tour as captain of the West Indies and a
reign which, once more, had seen the West Indians emerge as an all-
powerful force in world cricket came to its finish, ironically enough, after
a rare defeat for the West Indians at Sydney at the end of yet another
victorious series. There was the drama, the excitement, the romance and
the disbelieving sadness which all appear together as a great figure walks
or, in Lloyd's case, ambles off the field for the last time and on into the
pavilion and the pages of history. A chapter had ended.

By then Australia were being captained by a slightly surprised Allan
Border who had been thrust into the job and, simply by doing his best,
was trying to show that he was up to it. But the talk was not of Border but
of his predecessor, Kim Hughes, who had begun the season in charge after
a short and successful tour of one-day internationals in India. The might
of West Indian fast bowling, against the fragile nature of Hughes himself,
brought him down after two Test Matches. Hughes had added to history's
long list of famous last words when, before the series against the West
Indies, he promised to leave the hook shot in the dressing room and
proceeded to give West Indian fine legs the time of their lives. His
situation was not helped by the long-established truth that a captain is
seldom better than the strength of his side; and dangerous undercurrents
in the uncharted seas of Australian administration further weakened his
position. At a press conference in the players' dining-room at the Gabba
in Brisbane after Australia had lost the Second Test, a tearful Hughes
resigned his commission.

The questions remain. Was he led to the brink and pushed? Did he have any alternative but to throw in his hand? Were the newspaper headlines and adverse comment too much for any man? Were the considerable forces ganged up against him behind the scenes and the figures who moved through the coffee shop and the corridors of the Sheraton Hotel that weekend in Brisbane too irresistible? Would a man with a different approach to life and to himself have been able to withstand the battering? Was Hughes, in the end, the victim of his own character? And, most important of all: was he ever really up to the job? If it should not have been given to him, why was it?

There were many imponderables and I would be surprised if anyone who was closely involved with the goings-on in Perth and Brisbane over that fortnight was particularly proud of the part he played – and this includes Hughes himself. Personal prejudice may have been satisfied in more than one quarter but subsequent events were to show that Hughes's departure did little to help Australia's immediate cricketing future, even allowing for that victory in Sydney where the pitch was the true Australian hero.

After Hughes had bidden his farewell, Border was summoned to take over and, after losing the Third Test in Adelaide, was able to escape with a draw in Melbourne, thanks to a brave 100 by Andrew Hilditch whose career lurches from a tenuous position in the Australian side to one of no greater certainty in his District side in Adelaide. He is another, like Hughes, who has turned the business of hooking fast bowlers into fine legs' hands into an art form.

Then came the Sydney Cricket Ground pitch, the middle-aged leg spin of Bob Holland, the orthodox left-arm spin of Murray Bennett, delivered from behind dark glasses, and the last gallant but vain attempt by Clive Lloyd to score a hundred for the first time at the Sydney Cricket Ground – and Australia's resulting victory. Apart from the Australians' ability to read the pitch better than the West Indians and to play two spinners, it was not a victory which meant a great deal although it gave Australian cricket a much needed lifeline.

Hughes may have wanted the Australian captaincy for all the wrong reasons, as his plentiful supply of enemies was quick to point out. He may have been over-keen on the kudos and the benefits which come with such an honour. In short, he probably wanted the job for what he could get out of it, rather than for what he could put into it. It was this which angered Ian Chappell so much. There are two sides to most stories, however, and Hughes's supporters would argue vigorously against this. What cannot be denied, though, is his naivety and lack of foresight in dealing with people and, most particularly, with his colleagues. Nonetheless, he was a tragic figure in all that followed, never able at any stage to help himself and being pushed from a job he had worked very hard to persuade people he should have been given in the first place.

He had come into the Australian side in 1977 when the Chappell era was moving into its second stage. Ian Chappell had resigned from the captaincy in 1975 after leading Australia to victory on their tour to England after the first World Cup. Greg Chappell took over against the West Indians in Australia in 1975–76 and marked his success by scoring a century each innings of the First Test in Brisbane. But Ian remained in the side and, in the second match of that series in Perth which the West Indies won by an innings, he made 156 in Australia's first innings, arguably the best innings he ever played for Australia. His influence in all quarters remained strong.

Although there was a Board of Control and a panel of Test selectors, it does not need any great imagination to realize how completely the engine-room of Australian cricket was fuelled and administered by the Chappell family. It was onto this scene that the apparently fresh-faced, fair-haired, Boy's Own-looking hero, Kim Hughes, made his appearance. A healthy consistency in the Western Australian side caught the selector's eye and he was taken to England with Greg Chappell's side in 1977.

Hughes was to receive the first massive blow to his long-term future early on that tour. Kerry Packer had decided to stage his own form of Test cricket after his Channel 9 television network had been refused exclusive rights to televise cricket by the Australian Cricket Board. Having made the decision, Packer moved fast and recruiting officers were soon busy in the different parts of the world. The Chappells, Dennis Lillee and Rod Marsh must have had plenty of say in deciding who should be asked to form the Australian World Series Cricket squad. When the story hit the papers in May 1977, while Greg Chappell's side was engaged in a game against Sussex at Hove, Hughes's name was conspicuously absent from the list of Australians who had signed for Packer. He himself has suggested that he was approached by the Packer organization, but that he turned them down, although evidence of this is hard to find.

Hughes had not endeared himself by his overall attitude to Lillee and Marsh in the Western Australian side although they both did their best to help him when he was new to the state captaincy and they would have passed on their innermost thoughts to the Chappells. Although Ian was no longer captain of Australia when Hughes became a Test player, he had the strongest personality of the four and he has never been one to mince his words or to hide his dislike of Hughes. He is likely to have hardened the hearts of those who listened and who were, anyway, leaning away from Hughes.

In retrospect, Hughes's future was preordained from the moment that that invitation to join World Series Cricket failed to drop through his letter-box. Not only did it confirm the hostility of those who, as events were to prove, had a considerable influence on the future of Australian cricket, but it also indirectly confirmed the friendship of an establishment which was desperate for allies on the field of play and which, ultimately, was to have a lesser influence than they would surely have liked. Hughes was rejected, on the one hand, and then taken on board by an opposition which was to lose out in the end. Unwittingly or not, he had become an intensely political figure and was always to remain so.

When World Series Cricket and the Australian Cricket Board made an uneasy peace in 1979 the establishment went to great lengths to stress how genuine and sincere was that peace; I fear there was little doubt that they protested too much. The World Series Cricket players returned to the Australian side and Greg Chappell was reappointed as captain. On the surface, nothing had changed from the pre-Packer days; beneath the surface the currents were strong. With apologies to Orwell, all cricketers were equal but some cricketers were more equal than others.

While the World Series cricketers were back in force, the Australian Cricket Board used Hughes as their establishment talisman. He was Greg Chappell's vice-captain, hardly a move which would have satisfied the World Series Cricket protagonists, but one which they had to accept as window-dressing at the very least. Hughes obviously found himself in an impossible situation. It would have been surprising if his advice had been either sought or accepted. In the end, who can blame him if he kept his own counsel? But did he ever do more than walk from third slip to third slip? Did he try – indeed, did he know enough about the game to try? There are views both ways. Did he try and come up with answers and, if he did, surely he would have wanted to communicate with his captain? He did not seem to do so very often but was the link between Chappell, at first slip, and Marsh, behind the stumps, unbreakable? It was certainly hard for him but I wonder if Hughes had the character to make sure that he was given a fair hearing out there on the field.

Then Greg Chappell became choosy and Hughes's job harder still. Chappell decided that he would rather stay at home and tend to his business interests than go on certain tours. Hughes, as vice-captain, took over on these occasions and was in charge of players, certainly his leading players, whose loyalties belonged to Chappell and World Series Cricket. Did those players always give Hughes their best? Did he try to get the best out of them in the best possible way? Who was talking to whom in the dressing-rooms and in the hotels? And whose advice counted for what? It was nearly impossible for Hughes and would have stretched the prophet Job, Don Bradman and Mike Brearley rolled into one.

Hughes took the Australian side to India in 1979–80, to England in 1981 and to Pakistan in 1982–83 when Dennis Lillee was also unavailable; yet the moment Hughes returned to Australian soil Chappell was brought back by the Australian Cricket Board.

When I arrived in Brisbane for the start of the Pakistan tour in October

1983 I was told emphatically, during the first match against Queensland, that, if a vote had been taken there and then of the members of the Board, Marsh would have been appointed. The debate was vibrant but behind closed doors. There can be little doubt that some intensive lobbying was carried out behind the scenes by the influential members of the Board. Marsh's reputation as a bit of a larrikin probably counted against him in the heartland of the establishment and when, in late November, the vote was taken Hughes had a majority. He, himself, heard the news at Northam, a country town north of Perth where the Pakistanis were playing a one-day game against a Western Australian country eleven.

The First Test Match was to start later in the week and while the Australian side gathered at the Perth Sheraton Hotel the new Chairman of the Australian Cricket Board, Fred Bennett, flew in from Sydney. Bennett was in a mildly embarrassing position for he had made no secret of his support for Marsh. Realizing that he had been out-voted in a democratic situation, however, he nobly decided that it was his job to come to Perth and tell the Australians that all squabbling must be put aside and that everyone must get behind Hughes. He spoke to the team at a breakfast-time meeting on the Wednesday. At that time Perth was still vibrating from Allan Bond's triumph in winning the America's Cup for Australia in Newport and it was still wearing its heart on its sleeve.

That evening, after spending the day at the nets, both sides and many others involved were invited to drinks and dinner at the Royal Perth Yacht Club, the new home of the America's Cup. Speeches of welcome were made and all the appropriate platitudes and clichés reserved for these occasions were faithfully trotted out. Then, just as everyone was settling back to enjoy the evening, angry voices were raised. The two antagonists were revealed as none other than Kim Hughes and Rod Marsh. Conversationally, at any rate, there were no holds barred as insults were traded and it became most unpleasant. It was ironical that one of those with the equivalent of a ring-side pew for this particular fight was the Chairman of the Australian Cricket Board himself, Fred Bennett. So much for his rallying call after breakfast that morning. Hughes cannot have gone to bed a happy man that evening.

Pakistan played their first ever five-match Test series in Australia without the bowling of their captain, Imran Khan, who was suffering from a stress fracture of the left shin. He had hoped that it would mend in time, but this was not to be. Zaheer Abbas took over the captaincy and, although Imran was able to play in the last two Test Matches, it was only as a batsman. Australia won the series comfortably enough and at the end of the Fifth Test Match Greg Chappell, Lillee and Marsh all announced their retirement from Test cricket. As a result, Hughes's position as captain seemed finally to be safe.

In September 1984 Australia went to India for that short tour of one-day international matches and emerged victorious; the result should have cemented Hughes even more firmly in the job. The Australians returned to collect themselves for the forthcoming series against Clive Lloyd's West Indians – still the most formidable side on earth.

By then another figure had appeared on the edge of the Australian cricket administration; he may have had an influence on the events of the next few weeks. Bob Merriman, a professional arbitrator by trade, had, for a while, been the Australian Cricket Board's disciplinary officer. When a player was reported for bad conduct his case was heard by Merriman who, if the culprit was found guilty, pronounced sentence. His sentences were seldom severe as one might expect from someone who, in real life, was a conciliator. At times one could not escape the conclusion that he identified too strongly with the Australian side. In 1984 he was appointed full-time manager of the Australians and he would have checked and paid the team's hotel bills on that short tour of India.

One would have expected Merriman to have returned home from his first overseas tour as manager of the Australian side eminently satisfied, especially with his captain. He returned with the side from India in October 1984 and, a few weeks later, solemnly read Hughes's hastily prepared statement of resignation to the assembled press in the dining-room at the Gabba. Of course, the fact that, as team manager, he read the statement does not mean that he agreed with its contents.

Looking back on that weekend in Brisbane, with the advantage of hindsight, it was clear that something important was going on. Several times I came across huddled groups of cricket administrators at corner tables in the Sheraton coffee shop and, doubtless, that was only a small part of it all. Much would have been happening in the rooms upstairs. Merriman was a man who expressed himself strongly on most cricketing matters and I have no doubt that he had plenty to say now. He was not a man, too, who liked to end up on the losing side for he was ambitious. But I am getting ahead of the story.

Having publicly foresworn the hook – Hughes's public statements had an unhappy way of rebounding on him – he gave Marshall catching practice at fine leg when Michael Holding bowled him a bouncer in the first innings of the First Test Match in Perth. The media jumped on him from a great height and in hobnail boots and Hughes, as he always did when under fire, looked like a little-boy-lost. The second innings did not go much better for him and the West Indies won massively by an innings inside four days. Now Hughes, the victor against Pakistan at the start of the year and the winner in India in the one-day competition, faced fiercer criticism than ever before, even though his opponents now were the West Indies – the best side in the world – and he no longer had the services of Greg Chappell, Lillee and Marsh. Suddenly, he was found to be unsuitable to captain Australia.

If publicly foreswearing the hook was plain stupid, getting out so soon afterwards was regarded as criminal; indeed it was made to seem almost traitorous and apparently told of a decisive lack of moral fibre. If Hughes's head was not on the platter, he was being led blindfold to the scaffold while the executioner sharpened his axe. I cannot remember another cricketer, let alone a captain, being brought down so suddenly and so decisively when no dramatic crime had been committed, yet I still have the uneasy feeling that Hughes was somehow being paid back for past attitudes. If I am wrong, he was surely treated abominably.

At the time I could not help but get the impression that the end of his captaincy had been carefully planned and, at the first signs of mortality displayed by Hughes, an inevitable process was set in motion. When the team for the Second Test in Brisbane was announced Hughes was still the captain, but the anti-Hughes bandwagon was fast gaining pace. I have no idea who knew what, or whether, the lobby of administrators who were hostile to Hughes found public outlet for their views. I suspect that they did, however, and that in certain places comment was, to say the least, 'informed'. Looking back on it, I suppose Hughes might have survived Brisbane although there must have been long odds against him surviving the series. I just wonder if anyone thought, when Hughes was appointed to the captaincy a year earlier, 'oh well, it's not the end, the West Indies will put that right next year'.

In Brisbane, Hughes found himself under intolerable personal pressure. It would have been difficult for anyone to handle although those prepared to clench their jaw, in the cricketing sense, would have tried to provide a clear and splendid answer. Hughes can be a likeable chap but he is perhaps not personally tough enough to stand and fight battles like that on his own. The West Indies again won in four days and, again, Hughes made no great impact with the bat and allowed himself to fall over the brink. When the match was over there were the traditional press conferences in the players' dining-room at the Gabba where the two captains took turns to meet the press. When it was Hughes's turn, he stood by pale, nervous, disconsolate and, ultimately, tearful while Bob Merriman read out his statement of resignation.

Hughes had apparently made up his mind to resign earlier in the day and it is surely reasonable to suppose that the team manager, along with the Chairman of the Board and the Executive Director, would have been let into the secret. During the day Merriman ran into an old friend and supporter who was the cricket writer for a Melbourne paper and also a close friend of Hughes. The cricket writer told Merriman that, with the result a foregone conclusion, he was leaving before the end of the match to catch an aeroplane back to Melbourne. While it would have been improper for the Australian manager to have spoken of Hughes's impending resignation, he might have been expected to warn an old friend that, in the circumstances, it would have been strongly in his best interests to remain where he was. Perhaps he found it too embarrassing to say something like that. Needless to say, the two are no longer soul mates. I have told the story as I know it and leave the reader to make up his own mind. I cannot help but feel that Hughes lost support in the critical stages in areas where he had every right to expect loyalty. His power-base suddenly evaporated. I hope I am wrong. If not, the whole affair becomes even more squalid.

I know that there were a number of people who rubbed their hands with glee at Hughes's departure. I was told, too, of conversations involving Hughes and his immediate predecessor, Greg Chappell, which took place behind the scenes and would hardly have helped the peace of mind of the chap who was still captain of Australia. In such delicate situations one has to be careful of repeating what amounts to hearsay. Unrepeatable though most of these conversations are, they have left me in not too much doubt that there were those working away at Hughes's character, trying to open up his self-doubts even further and, in effect, giving him the final push.

At the end of it all one question still remains. Is a chap who reacted as Hughes did to the considerable pressures put on him, fit to captain Australia? I would suggest that there have been less successful Test captains who have never come within a hundred miles of experiencing the sort of pressure put on Hughes that weekend in Brisbane. Having said all that I am not, and never have been, convinced that Hughes had it in him, either as a man or as a thinker about the game (or, indeed, as a handler of his fellow cricketers), to be the answer to Australia's captaincy problems. What must be true, though, is that he never had a fair chance. Whether he deserved to be given the job remains in doubt; once he had it though, he should have been better supported.

While Hughes fell off the stage at Brisbane, Clive Lloyd's giant strides took him into Test history in vastly different circumstances at the Sydney Cricket Ground early in 1985. Those much operated-on knees, the exaggerated shuffle, the Paddington Bear look-alike and that huge bat which resembled, more than anything else, an animated tree trunk raised to the skies, departed to a memorable standing ovation after an innings of 72 which somehow managed to encapsulate all that was vibrant, thoughtful, semi-apologetic and technically brilliant about his batting. The feeling of limp anti-climax after he had gone was almost as strong as the thrill of his batting and the drama of his departure. Lloyd had his opponents, although I doubt they were many, but he was a great West Indian cricketer and a captain who gave purpose to the aspirations of all cricketing West Indians dotted about as they are all over the Caribbean in those unforgettable West Indian islands – these days, all individual island nations, which become the West Indies only for the purposes of cricket – and as expatriates in many other parts of the world.

I first saw the young Clive Lloyd walk out to bat at the Queen's Park Oval in Port of Spain, Trinidad, in January 1968, peering myopically through his glasses and looking, for all the world, like a character out of *Alice in Wonderland* who had lost his way. Who was he? Well, we were soon to find out. Those off drives peeled off his bat like orchestrated and elegant claps of thunder. Later in the covers he defied both the laws of logic and gravity for his knees had not yet encountered the surgeon's knife. At that time Gary Sobers was the king and yet, by the time Lloyd had ended his long career, he seemed, if anything, more of a father figure to West Indian cricket than even Sobers. That may, in part, have been because Sobers captained a West Indian side which was just starting to decline when he took over from Frank Worrell, for age was taking its toll. When his turn came, Lloyd took a young side, lifted it, set it down on top of the cricketing world and held it there until that day he set off for the pavilion for the last time in a Test Match.

Lloyd's ability as a batsman was underlined by 7,515 runs in 175 innings in Test cricket; as a captain he was good, but quite how good will never be known. He began in India in 1974–75 when West Indies won an exciting series by three matches to two. Then he came to Australia a year later with a bunch of raw talent which was as awesome as it was undisciplined. In that series in 1975–76 his batsmen were destroyed by Lillee and Thomson just as the Englishmen had been a year earlier. Viv Richards and Gordon Greenidge were still cutting their teeth at this level of the game while Andy Roberts and Michael Holding were only beginning to set up their fast bowling partnership. The six-Test series ended in a massive defeat for the West Indies by five matches to one. But, even so, there were, in this series, one or two overwhelming pointers to the future.

The West Indies won the toss in the Second Test Match in Perth and, in one of the most extraordinary exhibitions of controlled strokeplay I can remember, reached 585. Roy Fredericks, always a dasher and with a square cut that reminded one of a medieval tenant at harvest-time doing his best with a sickle, made 169 in an innings which will forever leap out of the score book for those who saw it. Clive Lloyd (149), Alvin Kallicharan, Derryck Murray and Keith Boyce all made contributions which, by only the acutest comparison, seem less frenetic.

It was an innings which was to have far-reaching effects for it prompted Johnny Woodcock, the cricket correspondent of *The Times*, and I, to decide over a plate of oysters that night at the Weld Club in Perth to drive a 1921 Rolls Royce from England to India in October 1976. After Fredericks, Roberts and Holding had the first of many joint successes in spite of the aforementioned 156 by Ian Chappell. The West Indies won by an innings and 87 runs. It was a foretaste of the Armageddon which was to come and, of all the crushing victories Lloyd's side achieved all over the world over the next decade, this one still stands out for me.

The next significant event took place in Hobart against Tasmania. Viv Richards had made a mere 12 in Perth and had not played a big innings in Australia. On that rather ancient but charming ground on the Domain overlooking Government House and the huge bridge over the Derwent Estuary, Lloyd sent Richards in first. He scored a hundred and started an endless procession of runs which, at the time of writing, has still not dried up. The remaining four Test Matches in that series in 1975–76 were all won by Australia and Lloyd's young men were as profligate with their talents as Sobers's ageing troopers had been in Australia seven years before. But the lesson was learned, England were annihilated in 1976 and the next eight years saw scarcely a mark on the debit side of the ledger for the West Indies.

The principal ingredient in their recipe for success was soon established. In the words of the cookery book it was 'add four fast bowlers and stir according to taste'. Not only was it an unstoppable combination but those lovely islands threw up a succession of fast bowlers, each of whom seemed to be faster and fiercer than the last. Roberts, Holding, Garner, Croft, Clarke, Walsh, Davis, Marshall, Gray, Patterson, Daniel – I daresay they could have found a dozen more if necessary. Two were bad enough, three were a real problem, four turned out to be game, set and match. England had done it once, under Douglas Jardine, in 1932–33 in Australia. To prevent it changing the game irrevocably the administrators then stepped in and made it impossible for a captain to set such an all-devouring leg-side field. Jardine had been allowed to have as many short legs as he wanted. Nowadays the Laws do not allow more than two fielders behind square on the leg side. It was the field placing which made the bodyline attack of Larwood and Voce so especially devastating, for they were able to bowl with three or more backward short legs and fielders behind them in the deep.

The West Indian quartet of fast bowlers changed the game. There are those who feel that Lloyd showed a cynical disregard for the traditions, niceties and accepted form of the game with this eternal barrage and lop-sided balance to his attack. I do not believe he did anything wrong in employing four fast bowlers for the West Indies have played the game within the Laws and, almost ten years on, in spite of the bleatings we have heard from their opponents, the Laws have remained unchanged. At times there have been too many bouncers but it is the umpires' job to sort that one out and they have seldom intervened. I cannot see why Lloyd should not have continued to play the game in a way which the authorities deemed to be legal.

Where Lloyd has been to blame, however, is in the matter of over-rates. The West Indians and their supporters become almost apoplectic when accused of using a slow over-rate as a deliberate tactical weapon. In a sense it is a chicken-and-egg situation for it is difficult to be sure whether these bowlers deliberately bowled at a slow rate or whether it just happened and then they became aware of the tactical advantage it gave them. When overs are bowled at around ten or eleven an hour it is impossible for the side batting second to score runs fast enough to give their own bowlers time enough to win the match if they are chasing a total much in excess of 350 or 400. If the side batting first makes around 400 and then bowls its overs at 11 or 12 an hour, the side batting second will not receive enough balls per hour to score runs fast enough to leave themselves time to bowl out the West Indians a second time and go on to win the match. This is a self-evident truth but it has almost certainly been self-interest by the West Indies which has been the main factor in preventing the International Cricket Conference from doing much more than pay lip-service to the problem. I am not saying that the West Indies are the only side to bowl their overs too slowly; this is a universal problem but, with their fast attack, it works more to their advantage to do so. Having said that, it must also be said that they have had some exceptional fast bowlers who would have won a great many matches whatever the over rate.

Lloyd successfully stage-managed an extraordinarily powerful side for nearly a decade. In so many ways he personified West Indies cricket and yet his powers of captaincy were never really tested. With the talent at his disposal things happened. During his last Test Match, at the Sydney Cricket Ground, I asked him in an interview for the BBC if, looking back over his long career, there was anything he regretted. He said quickly that he would like to have had New Zealand over again. The West Indies toured New Zealand early in 1980 and this was the only time they lost a Test series between 1976 and 1984. It was also one of the most bitter and unpleasant series ever to have been played, certainly since the bodyline series in 1932–33 and before England's visit to Pakistan in 1987–88.

The West Indies came on from Australia without Viv Richards who was injured and had to return home. Problems began immediately for they complained about their hotel accommodation in Hamilton where they played their first match and they went on to lay their failure to beat the New Zealanders at the door of the New Zealand umpires. There were the most unfortunate incidents on the field when appeals were turned down. For example, with a ballet dancer's flourish, Michael Holding kicked down the stumps when he had been thwarted in one appeal; with the swift footwork of a boxer Colin Croft barged into umpire, Fred Goodall, as he ran in to bowl. Because they were not getting their way the West Indians felt that the umpires were not being fair. The worst complaint they could have legitimately levelled at the New Zealand umpires was that one or two, Goodall in particular, were over-officious and that there were on occasions disturbing levels of incompetence; but they were not dishonest.

The situation was not helped by Willie Rodriguez, the West Indian manager who, by all accounts, was disgracefully ineffectual and not much more than a lackey of the players. His refusal to try to bring his players into line was as shameful as their actions on the field. Lloyd himself opted out. He did not want to know and said and did nothing at the time. His players decided in the middle of one Test Match that they were going home and only frantic telephone calls between New Zealand and Port of Spain, Trinidad (at the time the headquarters of the West Indian Cricket Board of Control) saved the tour.

Lloyd regretted deeply all that had happened. On the other hand, Rodriguez compounded his weaknesses when, at the time of England's confrontation in Pakistan with umpire Shakoor Rana in late 1987, he was rung up by a London newspaper and asked about the incidents in New Zealand. He said that the New Zealanders were only paying the West Indies back for wrongs that they, the New Zealanders, felt they had suffered in the Caribbean in 1971–72. I happened to see every match on that particular tour – many more than Rodriguez – and the New Zealand players managed to survive all five Test Matches and drew the series 0–0. They should really have lost at least two Tests and not only had little cause for complaint but did not make a great fuss either.

The West Indies did not emerge with any credit from the tour of New Zealand and nor did Lloyd. It was a situation in which a strong captain would surely have taken control and switched his players' minds back to the job of playing cricket and winning, or have sent one or two home. Instead of which, Lloyd stood by as others orchestrated the crisis and he allowed them to take charge.

If Lloyd, the captain, was an enigma, Lloyd the batsman was one of the more marvellously exciting players I have seen. His centuries were always memorable and his means of execution was prehensile. No one has ever hit a cover drive with greater power or a hook more resoundingly and yet he still produced those delightful, improvised touches which, perhaps more than anything, bore testimony to the strength of his arms and wrists with that heavy bat. Lloyd had a rare touch at the crease and was never for a single second dull. With that shuffle that grew more pronounced with old age he became an increasingly homely figure.

I shall not forget his final Test innings in Sydney. The West Indies were doomed on that turning pitch. Lloyd came in, head stretched forward, looking studious to the last. He pushed thoughtfully up and down the line for a few exploratory overs. Then, that massive right pad came thrusting up the pitch, that huge willow tree up in the air behind him and woof – down it came and the ball shot through the covers and raced back twenty yards onto the outfield off the pavilion rails. We all knew it was his final Test innings and it was a relief to see him get off the mark and a joy to savour every stroke, whether in defence or attack. It was like drinking the last bottle of a great vintage.

Suddenly, fifty was a possibility and, if fifty, why not that elusive hundred which had always eluded him at the Sydney Cricket Ground? His half-century arrived and was appropriately saluted. Still his cover drive split the field as he chewed rhythmically and phlegmatically on a long-suffering piece of chewing gum. Then Craig McDermott ran in again, Lloyd leant forward into the drive, the ball was not quite there and Border gratefully accepted a low skimming catch at extra cover. And that was the end of Lloyd.

— 2 —
Cricket's Irresistible Force

Gower takes over, 1984–86 • Gower succeeds Willis as England
captain • motivating Botham the Brearley way • a broken
nose for Gatt • West Indies 1985–86 • 'optional practice' and
supine management • visa problems for Boycott and
Engel • anti-apartheid demonstrations melt away • the
Edmonds double act • fast bowling and the media demoralize
England • Antigua unhappy about Gooch • the enigma that
is Gower • who would choose to be an England captain?

Australia and the West Indies were not the only countries to have
captaincy problems in 1984 and 1985. England had begun the year with
Bob Willis in charge in New Zealand and Pakistan, but he became ill in
Pakistan and David Gower led the side in the last two Test Matches.
Willis's captaincy had not been a success; it is not often a bowler does the
job well, especially if he is a fast bowler. He was appointed by Peter May,
his first act after becoming chairman of the selectors in 1982. Keith
Fletcher had taken the side to India in 1981–82 and, by all accounts, had
not done a bad job although the series was lost. May, taking charge for the
first time, felt that it was necessary to inject a new attitude and approach
into the side and that Fletcher was, by and large, too negative a character;
in addition, there had been quite a hullabaloo when Fletcher had flipped
off his bails when given out in one Test Match, caught off bat and pad
close to the wicket in a questionable decision when he did not think that he
had hit the ball. In this series the umpiring caused problems and Fletcher's
dissent may have been too much for the new chairman of selectors. He has
grown less squeamish since.

To many of us reporting the England tour from Pakistan, Willis's
illness was a gift from heaven for it presented a solution to a problem
which had appeared to founder on selectorial obstinacy. It was, I dare say,
wishful thinking on our part to praise Gower's performances during the
last two Test Matches as lavishly as we did. A Pakistan wicket fell in the
Faisalabad Test, a forward short leg and a silly point were brought up, the
two batsmen suddenly found themselves under pressure and Mudassar
was caught at silly point. When you think about it, it was elementary and
perhaps our cries that, at last, England had a captain who was prepared to

try and make things happen rather than simply waiting in the hope that something would turn up were, no doubt magnified out of proportion through sheer relief. In the final Test in Lahore, when a splendid innings by Shoiab Mohammad looked like making a mess of a carefully planned declaration, Gower, with principal support from his then Leicestershire colleague, left-arm spinner, Nick Cook, indulged in as reprehensible an exhibition of time-wasting as any I have seen and, as a result, hung onto an ill-deserved draw.

By then the whole tour was in turmoil because of drug-taking allegations made against Ian Botham and others while they were in New Zealand on the first leg of the tour. I have dealt with this particular saga at some length in *One Test After Another*. It is enough to say that the influx of newshounds from Fleet Street, the constant stream of newspaper headlines and endless telephone calls between the tour management in Pakistan and Lord's could only have had an unsettling effect. To make matters worse, Sarfraz Nawaz, the old Pakistan fast bowler, made some extraordinary accusations against Botham which, to say the least, would have been hard to prove. Botham himself returned home with an injury which, whether diplomatic or real, took some of the pressure off those still in Pakistan. But as soon as he returned to England he told reporters that Pakistan was a place where mothers-in-law should be sent on a compulsory all-expenses' paid trip. It endeared him even less to his most recent hosts and eventually he was fined for these remarks by the TCCB.

Gower did not, therefore, have Botham to contend with in either of his first two Test Matches as captain. Former captains can be difficult to handle for they are bound to have ideas of their own. Botham has always had ideas of his own: some extravagant, some stupid, some good and some which I daresay bordered on farce. Mike Brearley had the ability to encourage him to keep the ideas flowing but he was also able to edit them. Although Brearley and Botham had their share of arguments, Brearley was always able to propagate, encourage and use his enthusiasm. After making two noughts in the Second Test against Australia at Lord's in 1981 Botham resigned the captaincy minutes before he was sacked.

Brearley was reappointed and eight days later led out an England team at Leeds which included Botham who, with important help from Willis, found the drive to turn what seemed to be certain defeat into an incredible victory for England. Brearley, a head shrinker by trade, had managed in a short space of time to create an atmosphere in the England dressing-room, and an attitude of mind in Botham himself, which put flesh and blood on what Ladbrokes, the bookmakers, considered to be a 500–1 chance.

No subsequent England captain was able to imitate Brearley's genius, and at times, Botham's vigorously expressed ideas in the slips were counter-productive to his side's course. If they were not acted upon he seemed at times to grow disenchanted and there have been occasions when he and his captains have been visibly at loggerheads. Of course, Botham's genius as a player has been an asset no captain could afford to be without but, in other ways, he was sometimes a mixed blessing as his huge and irrepressible personality and ego tried to take over.

By his own standards Botham had a quiet series against the West Indies and, until the time of writing, he has never been at his best against them. By the time these words are read he should have had another chance to put this particular record straight – in England in 1988 – but the operation on his back put paid to that. In fact, in the series in England in 1984 his figures were not too bad for he scored 347 runs at an average of just under thirty-five and he took nineteen wickets at an average of just over 35. It was greatly to Gower's credit that he managed to get as much out of Botham as he did but, of course, there was never the slightest chance that he was going to be able to reproduce the feats that enabled Brearley's side to beat the Australians back in 1981, simply because the West Indians were such a formidable outfit.

At times in '84 against the West Indies Gower did, I thought, a pretty good job but, at other times, it was as though he found this supernatural force ranged against him almost beyond his comprehension and he appeared not to know what to do. Perhaps on those occasions he should have looked more to the chairman of the selectors for his help and advice. It was not a glorious summer for English cricket, by any means, but there was no earthly point in sacrificing a captain at this stage for losing 5–0 to the West Indies; the series may have been a little uglier than it should have been but defeat was, for all that, unavoidable. It was an experience that those in charge would have hoped that Gower should have benefited from and become a better captain as a result of it.

During the Fourth Test of that series at Old Trafford Botham announced that, for family reasons, he would not be available for the 1984–85 tour of India. Obviously, no side could view the absence of Botham the cricketer with anything other than alarm but the absence of Botham the man was perhaps a different matter. The previous March he had made it abundantly clear what he felt about visiting Pakistan and, indeed, the sub-continent in general. If England had been going anywhere else but India that winter he might have taken a different view. As it was, his absence made it certain that the tour would not be played with the incidents that Botham has a knack of causing. It also meant that Gower, on his first full tour as captain, would not have to cope with an influence which could, at times, be all too counter-productive.

It is easier to build up a good team spirit in tours of India and Pakistan than elsewhere for the team is thrown together, more than on any other tour, as there are fewer alternatives to the team room in the evenings. In some of the more remote venues the facilities are not all that they might be and a little bit of shared discomfort usually brings everyone together. On a tour of Australia the team room in the hotel can be empty for nights on end and the dressing-room then becomes the only regular gathering place. By all accounts, Gower's side developed an excellent spirit in India which was reflected in their cricket for, after losing the First Test Match in Bombay, they went on to win the series. Mike Gatting, Tim Robinson and Neil Foster were outstanding, Gower himself played well and handled the side intelligently and should have returned home much more confident in his new job.

1985 was another Australian summer and, although a marvellous 196 by Allan Border and some delightful leg-spin bowling by Bob Holland took Australia to their customary victory at Lord's, England, with Botham restored to the side, won the series 3–1. By the end of the summer they had reduced their opponents to the point of disintegration. Robinson, Gatting, Gower and Gooch all made big scores and, by the time September arrived, victory in the forthcoming series in the West Indies was even being contemplated. England's cricket seemed in good order and in the capable hands of a captain who had just won successive series against India and Australia.

Yet the series in the West Indies was an unmitigated disaster for England who lost 5–0, for Gower whose captaincy was poor and whose seemingly casual approach told decisively against him, and for Botham who had an unsuccessful tour on the field and whose antics off it kept him continually on the front page of the tabloids as one scandal unfolded after another. The details were remarkable enough to deserve the next chapter all to themselves. The disruptive effect on an already beleaguered side must not be underestimated. There was also the presence of Graham Gooch who, after his recent excursions to South Africa, was not everyone's favourite guest around the Caribbean, most especially in Trinidad whose government surprisingly seemed to withdraw support for the tour when it had already begun. On the field the inevitable collection of four West Indian fast bowlers and their quite devastating effect seemed almost irrelevant to the goings-on away from the cricket. There can have been few more disastrous cricket tours.

It all began on a pitch in Kingston which had some pace and a shockingly uneven bounce; Patrick Patterson, the newest fast-bowling recruit, destroyed England's batting. Mike Gatting tried to hook Malcolm Marshall in the first one-day international shortly before the Test Match and left on the next aeroplane for London without a bridge to his nose. It was clear well before the end of this first Test Match that another 5–0 drubbing was more than just a faint possibility. The West Indian attack was unrelenting; nerves, techniques, temperament and the will to fight were all tested and most were found wanting. Probably the best England could have looked forward to after leaving Kingston was to hold on for a couple of draws; even that was going to call for massive discipline on the part of batsmen who first had to make sure they did not get out playing strokes at balls they could safely leave alone.

Hard work in practice to eradicate this fault was a necessity, but, instead of this, we now found ourselves living in a land of 'optional practice', a phrase which must have come back to haunt Gower who was apparently content that his players should either have nets or go out on boat trips round the Caribbean. The manager was, once again, Tony Brown, who, as the tour became increasingly difficult on and off the field, seemed to have less and less control. The cricket manager was Gower's immediate predecessor, Bob Willis, and his appointment can only be described as less than inspired. He had been captain the year before and was therefore much too close to the players and, in any event, his own brand of leadership had never been that inspiring. Gower needed more positive support just as his principal all-rounder needed stronger control.

The loss of Gatting and the First Test was bad enough and the pointers were hardly encouraging. In Trinidad the anti-apartheid campaigners were making plenty of noise and it seemed that the Chambers government, which had accepted the tour in principle, was now having second thoughts. The upside-down Hilton – the entrance hall is on the top floor – in Port of Spain had a massive armed guard round it while the England players were there. Ironically, perhaps, it was not the English cricketers but the journalists who felt the first brunt of hardening Trinidad opinion. On the evening the First Test ended in Kingston two of the press corps, Geoffrey Boycott who had reluctantly been lured to substitute pen for willow on behalf of the *Daily Mail*, and Matthew Engel whose happy turn of phrase and considerable wit regaled the columns of the *Guardian*, set forth, unprepared, for Port of Spain.

When they arrived they found a determined immigration official demanding to see their visas for Trinidad and Tobago. Of course, neither they nor anyone else had visas for the excellent reason that, in the past, no one had ever needed visas to visit Trinidad and Tobago and the government had never made public any change of policy. Engel and Boycott landed in Port of Spain at Piarco Airport soon after midnight – not the time of day when these issues are best sorted out. Worried telephone calls brought officials from the British High Commission scurrying to the airport and, after much consultation, Boycott and Engel, an unlikely couple, were driven under police guard to Port of Spain's Holiday Inn Hotel and spent the night with the constabulary poised in the corridors outside their rooms. Their telephones were not cut off, however, and so they were able to alert their offices in London, and also the rest of us who were still enjoying the flesh-pots of Kingston, as to what awaited us on the morrow.

It was with mild apprehension to say the least that we approached our aeroplane the next afternoon for the flight to Port of Spain. When we arrived immigration officials were out in force and, happily, there was a fair sprinkling of High Commission staff. Eventually, we were allowed into the country but only after each of us agreed to pay a sizeable sum and to surrender our passports. We were promised that they would, in time, be returned with the appropriate visas. Tired, bedraggled and irritated we struggled into the Hilton Hotel looking, with apologies to Jean Rook who was later to join the tour briefly in Antigua, like a number of badly crumpled British West Indian Airways blankets. No matter where you are, if your hosts start off with an overt display of bad manners, suspicion spreads and one adopts the attitude of 'What is next on the agenda?'

In cricketing terms we had a welcome break when a brilliant hundred by Graham Gooch enabled England to win a most unlikely victory off the last ball in the one-day international in Port of Spain. The police in and around the hotel were bristling with every sort of weapon but, mercifully, they never had the slightest need to pull the triggers. The only other danger appeared to be a perpetual bunch of students who marched round the Queen's Park Oval chanting 'Nelson Mandela' and spending rather more of their time at the back of the commentary boxes than anywhere else. They were also closely watched by a number of police.

The Test Match came next and produced another annihilation for England. The crowds were not big and the demonstrators seemed to lose interest. With each day their numbers dwindled, although the faithful few still did their best with Nelson Mandela. Gooch's 100 in the one-day match had, of course, taken some of the sting out of this particular situation for he had played the sort of innings that can only bring joy to a West Indian heart and it had been highly appreciated by a very reasonable crowd.

The Botham dramas began in Port of Spain when his then manager, Tim Hudson, the former Los Angeles disc jockey who, of course, was born in England, said in California that 'of course Botham smokes pot. Everyone smokes pot and what of it?' David Gower had an equally insensitive swim with a British Airways hostess in the pool of the Hilton Hotel in full view of the rest of the world. Botham sat beleaguered in his hotel bedroom and manager Tony Brown strode about trying to look purposeful without really succeeding. Scarcely a journalist arrived at the side of the pool without a story to tell and the only humour (mercifully there was plenty of it too) came from Mr and Mrs Phil Edmonds. Mr Edmonds strode around in that stage-managed, world-weary way of his suggesting that it was only from the goodness of his heart that he had left his world of tycoonery to lend a hand in the Caribbean in the first place and was beginning to think that he had made the wrong decision.

Mrs Edmonds was a new phenomenon with ever-twinkling eyes, an irresistible smile and a nose with antennae which left no stone unturned. She was the wife on tour writing a book. Although she had her ear close to the ground life was not simple as she had to share a room with Mr

Edmonds, an experience not necessarily conducive to good authorship. He is an insomniac who clambers around his room all night with the lights on in the relentless pursuit of coffee. Mrs Edmonds has trained in a hard school, however, for she spends much of her time working in Brussels as an interpreter for the Common Market and has lived, therefore, her particular 'yes minister' form of existence for some years. If you twist her arm I suspect she will own up to speaking fluently at least three completely unknown languages as well as about twenty known ones. Her task was to write a light, racy, amusing account of the lady wife on tour. In my view she did it brilliantly and, with her force of personality, managed to convert into friends several who set out to knock her. Not everyone can persuade Fleet Street to change direction, especially if it is from hate to love. I found her an enormous asset as I am sure does Mr Edmonds if he is able, from time to time, to pause to consider her in his relentless chase for mega-bucks. Mrs E's final product, *Another Bloody Tour*, was my sort of tour book in a one-off way. It is sad to think that Mr E's deliberate demise as an international cricketer in 1987 may well have put the stopper on Mrs E's admirable pen. We can but keep our fingers crossed although, of course, we are getting ahead of the story.

Having said all that, I am quite certain that other less worldly cricketing wives might not find Mrs E wholly to their liking and, I daresay, one or two players with less imagination than some might not have fully appreciated the joke. But while Mrs E managed at times to turn our minds from the cricket – goodness knows we needed that badly enough – not even she was able to improve it although she undoubtedly had the great advantage of being able to ignore it.

England flew from Trinidad to Barbados for the Third Test only to find the island had been taken over by a great many English cricket supporters who spent the next fortnight growing more and more depressed, saying less than complimentary things about England's cricketers and, at the same time, showing how desperately painful, blistery and red hastily acquired suntan can be. I saw bodies of all shapes and sizes, beginning their visit to Barbados a whiter shade of pale, who went through the full spectrum of torture until they finished as fully paid-up members of Dante's *Inferno*. And they must have paid the earth for this self-inflicted torture.

England's cricketers, meanwhile, were completely rudderless and the practice sessions in Barbados were more optional than ever. There is good reason to say that sides who are playing constant cricket on tour can have too much net practice. On the other hand, a side which is being destroyed needs to try to do something for its own morale and, indeed, for the morale of its many hundreds of supporters. It needs to be seen to be trying to put things right. Public relations is, on these occasions, an important exercise. Practices at Kensington Oval should have been whole-hearted and compulsory although they need not have continued for twenty-four hours a day. A few arrived at the nets to turn their arms over, some preferred the beach, others may have looked no further than rum and Cokes and some may have hired cars or mopeds and scooted around the island. A nice holiday and a reasonable approach if you're winning 2–0 but, when you're on the receiving end of a thrashing which looked more and more as if it would end up at 5–0, it is ill-conceived madness or, I suppose, a premature chucking-in of the towel. It was all made doubly unhappy when England's batting in the Bridgetown Test Match was bad even by its own newly acquired standards.

As I say, the disaster was made to seem even worse as there were, in the crowd, at least 4,000 Englishmen who were holidaying in Barbados. A splendid innings of 160 by Richie Richardson took the West Indies to 418 in their first innings and, at the close on the second day, Gooch and Gower batting very well had taken England to 110 for one. It looked that evening as if the England batsmen had at last got the measure of the fast bowlers. Joy could hardly have been more short-lived. The next day England lost their last nine wickets for 79 and again followed on. Worse was to come for, by the close of play, six of the second-innings wickets had also gone down and the West Indies had won by an innings and 30 runs ten minutes before lunch on the fourth day. It is true that the pitch had an uneven bounce and the seam bowlers found plenty of movement but, all the same, the batting was bad. Batsmen were continually out to balls there was no need to play at and, even after Gooch and Gower's splendid example on the second evening, there was a sad and noticeable lack of determination by the remainder.

Of course, there is nothing that saps the morale of batsmen more than a constant barrage of short-pitched fast bowling. It wears down nerves and, in the end, destroys techniques. What had happened at Kensington Oval, Barbados, did not do much for the 'optional practice' theory. Maybe the management had already decided that England were in the grip of an irresistible force. If they had, they had no business to do so that early in the tour.

After Barbados, the Fourth Test in Trinidad and the Fifth in Antigua were a foregone conclusion and the West Indies won by ten wickets and 240 runs respectively. England had to suffer a final brilliant insult in Antigua when, in the West Indies' second innings, Viv Richards scored the fastest century in the history of Test cricket. He took just fifty-six balls to reach three figures, beating J.M. Gregory, the Australian, who had scored 100 against South Africa at Johannesburg from sixty-seven balls in 1921–22. One will be lucky if, in a lifetime, one sees again an innings which combined a magnificent brutality with an awe-inspiring brilliance and a disdainful contempt which seems to be the prerogative of Richards when he is at his very best. He was Gulliver among the Lilliputians.

This time it would have been futile and fanciful to blame England's captain who stuck his chin out and, in the first innings, scored 90, the highest individual score by an Englishman in the series. Although Gower may have looked uninterested at times and downtrodden at others, he was much the most successful batsman during the series as a whole. After that final humiliation in Antigua England's bowlers could not catch the aeroplane home quickly enough and the batsmen were not far behind. No Test side can ever, in the history of cricket, have been so completely demolished and demoralized.

By the time the side left Barbados after that dreadful defeat in the Third Test Match the Botham saga was in full swing with Mick Jagger and Jerry Hall watching the match from the Challoner stand at the Kensington Oval. Sticking at the moment to cricketing matters, another problem which threatened to blow the tour apart was quietly simmering from Barbados onwards. Graham Gooch had, in the first place, made himself available for the tour with some reluctance. As he went round the West Indies the pressure on him increased because of his South African excursion with the England rebel side – which, of course, he captained. He wasted no opportunity to let people know that he did not want to be in the West Indies and would infinitely prefer to be back at home which, although maybe understandable, hardly did wonders for the team spirit. Gooch, the man, was never less than gloomy. Gooch, the batsman, except for that one-day match in Port of Spain, was little more than Gooch going through the motions. With Tim Robinson's already fragile technique outside the off stump having been blown to smithereens, England always seemed to be two wickets down for not very many.

Earlier in the tour Gooch had read a statement written by the Antiguan Foreign Minister, Lester Bird, condemning South Africa in a way Gooch felt was unacceptable; he contemplated not going to Antigua unless the Foreign Minister retracted his statement. An impasse seemed to have been reached and Gooch is not a man who changes his mind lightly. Donald Carr, as Secretary of the Test and County Cricket Board, flew out to Port of Spain from Lord's and a series of meetings went on at the Hilton Hotel from which people emerged from time to time talking as often as not behind the backs of their hands. Whether it was the result of the gentle art of diplomacy or the altogether fiercer routine of the press-gang, Gooch boarded the aeroplane for Antigua where England suffered, as we have seen, another massive defeat.

Although David Gower had come to the West Indies with his confidence boosted by that victory in India and also by the defeat of the Australians in England, it was soon clear that this tour was an altogether different proposition. If he had been spared the troubles off the field and had had behind him a strong management and if, as it should have been, a more appropriate side had been picked in the first place, he might have managed to draw a couple of matches. For all that, he seemed to decide much too early that he was in the hands of some *force majeure*. As captain, he appeared to give up in spite of his success as a batsman.

It is interesting to speculate on what might have happened if Gower had had the advice and support of Micky Stewart who, later in the year, was to become the permanent England cricket manager and was such a help to Mike Gatting on the tour of Australia in 1986–87, although with Stewart close familiarity with the job and the players did not in the end serve him too well as we see later. There is no doubt that Gower was unlucky to face a second West Indian explosion; there is equally no doubt that he did not give himself his best chance. But, as we shall see in a moment, that is Gower's way. If he is ever to come back to the job as England's captain he must show that he is more obviously prepared to try to tackle the problems that face him.

Outwardly, Gower has always been an enigmatic figure and his captaincy has to be seen in terms of his character. He has that lissom, seemingly careless grace, the prerogative of so many left-handers; Graeme Pollock and Gary Sobers were two others whom I saw, and then there was Frank Woolley who, by all accounts, had it in greater abundance than anyone. You have only to see Gower take a few steps from the pavilion to realize that you're in the presence of an extraordinary athlete. His walk is loose-limbed, yet balanced to perfection, there is about him an air of studied, ambling inconsequentiality and the effect is to make you sit up and take notice. Those first few steps out of the pavilion have told similar stories about other fine cricketers. A batsman's walk is often indicative of the way in which he bats.

There is nothing in the least urgent in Gower's appearance as a cricketer. Even when stretching to make his ground and avoid a run out he gives the impression of being less than desperately bothered by the outcome. This casual exterior spills over into his captaincy and, as he walks from first slip to first slip or mid-off to mid-off between overs, or even when engaged in moving the field or changing the bowling, this same easy-going aura is there. The irony is that it all paints a false picture of Gower the man, Gower the cricketer and Gower the captain. There is no one who is more concerned, no one more eager to make that run, no one more worried about his side's lack of success and no one who is more browned off at being stuck with a label of being a chap whose life is based on a shrug of the shoulders philosophy.

He has been extremely disturbed by the interpretation which has been so commonly put upon his cricket and his captaincy, but he has been unable to change outward appearances. In England in 1986, after the disastrous tour of the Caribbean, he was given the England captaincy for two Test Matches against India with a clear warning from the chairman of the selectors, Peter May, that he had to make himself seen to be more involved in the game, to make it demonstrably clear that he was the captain and to lead from the front. Gower was all too aware of what was expected of him and even joked about it, saying that he supposed he should go out wearing a shirt with the words, 'I am the captain', on the back of it. As it happened, nothing much changed and when India won the Second Test Match at Lord's Gower was sacked and Gatting took over. With a sense of humour which is rare on these occasions Gower presented his successor with his tee-shirt which actually said, 'I'm in charge'.

I became fully aware of how much Gower minded and, contrary to popular opinion, thought about it all in late October 1986 when he travelled with six of us by train across the Nullarbor Plain from Adelaide to Kalgoorlie early in the tour of Australia. He had by then lost the captaincy and was going through a dreadful spell with the bat and had not even been included in the general tour committee. But again that is getting ahead of the story. As we have seen, Gower's appearance is deceptive. If he lacks anything it is probably self-confidence; this may seem strange in one who bats as if he is overflowing with it. Gower is shy and slightly reticent by nature. You could hardly have, for example, two more contrasting figures in a dressing-room than Gower and Botham. But because Gower is reticent and is not a confident captain as, say, Mike Brearley, it does not mean that he does not think any less intently, although his thoughts may not be so incisive and he finds a solution harder to find. Lack of confidence is one reason why he may take longer than he should to put his thoughts into action. His so casual attitude gives a strong impression that he really is not too concerned about what is going on around him.

As a rule unsuccessful and apparently unimaginative captains do not change their ways and return after a period out of office to produce similar results and solutions as before. I have a feeling that Gower might be an exception to this. He did the job in his own way as best he could and, having been sacked, will have carried out a strict self-examination. Gower is intelligent enough to know where he got it wrong and to realize that, if you are not producing the results, outward appearances are important for they will be accepted at face value.

Gower won back the Leicestershire captaincy from Peter Willey, who had kept it for only a year, before the start of the 1988 season. After his finger-wagging exercise in Pakistan Gatting's grip on the England job was surely less than firm and in no time at all that invitation to a waitress to have a late-night drink in his bedroom during the First Test against the West Indies had completely dished him. At the start of the season one did not have to stretch the imagination too far to see Gower eventually back in charge. He had a winter away from cricket in 1987–88 and the hope was that it had rejuvenated him. Alas for England, his batting was so terrible that by the time the Fifth Test against the West Indies came round he had been dropped. By then John Emburey, Chris Cowdrey and, because of an injury to Cowdrey, Graham Gooch had all had the chance to discover that captaincy against the West Indies is not an easy job. At the end of a ridiculous summer few things can have mattered less than the possibility of Gower mending his ways. For all that, I can still see him one day being a worthwhile captain of England.

Test captaincy these days is, in so many ways, a thankless task. The media focus attention on a captain as never before, lauding him to the heavens if all goes well, berating him, often beyond the realms of reason, if it goes badly and sitting in wait for him at all times. Very few captains are better than the side they lead. Failure is put under the microscope and, although a captain may be in charge of an extremely poor team, a consistent lack of success is eventually blamed on the man in charge. No captain will be sacked if he wins and, in the modern age, none will survive a constant trail of defeat.

This reaction to defeat must, in large part, have bred the modern safety-first approach of almost all contemporary captains. It is an 'avoid defeat at all costs' philosophy. Never take a chance until the odds are so stacked in your favour that it is no longer a risk. Delay your declaration so that nothing except a thunderbolt or a declaration of war will allow your opponents to win. Be content to stuff up a cricket match rather than show enterprise and lay down a challenge which would produce a splendid game but make defeat a realistic possibility. These days, fielding captains are not prepared to try to buy wickets, to give away runs in the hope of picking up a wicket or two by making the batsman careless. They refuse to realize that, to give yourself the best chance of victory, you often have to give the opposition a chance of victory too.

With so much importance attached to winning, these attitudes have also become prevalent in club cricket. How much harder to disturb them at first class, let alone Test, level. There is, in all this, a classic catch 22 situation. All captains need the confidence their own success will bring them, but they do not have the confidence to go out and give themselves their best chance of gaining that success. I daresay this will remain while defeat is regarded as such a humiliating disgrace. This then brings us to the financial rewards for the players. Victory earns a better pay packet than defeat. Is it surprising that captains are not prepared to gamble with their own or their players' weekly envelope? It's a hell of a job.

Of course, there are exceptions like Mike Brearley who was able to take two steps backwards and look at the job as an intellectual exercise. Then there are the Richie Benauds, the Ray Illingworths and the Ian Chappells who have brought their considerable skills and cunning to a difficult job. There will always be exceptions and all of us who have played cricket at any level have a captain we admire, for whatever reason. But these are the exceptions that prove the rule. A captain needs to be general, adjutant, sergeant-major, barrack-room lawyer and spy all rolled into one. And it would help if he had done ten years in the War Office before that. Even then, he may be unprepared to cope with the sort of problems that faced Gatting in Pakistan where the only answer can ever be to 'turn again the other cheek'. No amount of finger wagging will ever persuade an umpire to change his mind or turn an enemy into a friend.

By now, captaining your country at cricket must seem to be about the worst job in the whole of sport. Why on earth can anyone be so stupid as to want it? Human nature provides the answer to that one. There are very few who are not anxious to climb to the top of the tree in their own profession. If they get to the top many enjoy the attention, applause and, maybe, hero worship. There are those, too, who feel that they can do the job better than the present incumbent or, indeed, any other pretender. They feel they can bring something to the job no one else can. They are sure they can bring the best out in those beneath them. Perhaps, too, they have a sneaking feeling that they can establish their names so that history will look back and congratulate them. One or two may be certain that they know how to win if they get the job. Finally, who would ever knowingly throw up the chance to captain their country at anything? Not you, or me for that matter, so we're always assured of a guy who will lead us out of the pavilion. What we're not too sure about is what will happen from then on.

— 3 —
A Troubled Life

Botham's Caribbean ructions 1985–86 • the 'Viv Richards factor' in his make-up • police allegations of drug misuse • talk of Hollywood stardom • tabloid sex and drugs sensation mongering • Botham retracts his previous denials.

In *One Test After Another* I went into all the difficulties which beseiged Ian Botham on the England tour of New Zealand and Pakistan in 1983–84 which, I'm afraid to say, he brought on himself. He has seldom been free from trouble since going to Australia as a Whitbread scholar in the mid-seventies (before playing cricket for England) and having a violent and much publicized argument with Ian Chappell in a bar in Melbourne. At some stage Chappell says, in his account of the events, that Botham deliberately broke a glass and went for Chappell with the broken jagged half. Botham enjoys alcohol but it has contributed to some of his worst excesses. There are times when he appears to be taken over by an outside force and the only way he then regards an argument is to settle it with clenched fists. For some years the cricket authorities have bent over backwards to accommodate Botham but he is an addictive character in that, whenever attracted by a new influence, he gives it everything.

I once had a public scrap with Botham in the transit lounge at Bermuda Airport on the flight back from the West Indies after England's defeat in 1980–81 when he was captain. I gave a blow-by-blow account of that much-publicized episode in *Caught Short at the Boundary*, or *Wine, Women and Wickets* as it was called in Australia. Since then, I think we have made our peace and, although our paths do not often cross in a personal sense, we seem to get on reasonably well. On a one-to-one basis I find him charming and I enjoy talking to him about his various country pursuits like shooting and fishing; on these occasions he is an excellent companion.

But he does get himself into some extraordinary fixes. There is obviously another side to him, a less attractive side when his personality and ego become overemphasized. I have never thought that there was anything deliberately evil in Botham. I don't think that he is that sort of chap but, undoubtedly, certain influences work on him to make him exaggeratedly mischievous – to say the least.

27

In this chapter I want to have a look at the public list of problems which affected him on Gower's tour of the West Indies for the good reason that they had an effect on all of us and cannot, therefore, be ignored. In the same way, later in this book I shall look at his behaviour in Australia which led to his being sacked by Queensland because it is impossible to ignore that at a time when boorish behaviour is sweeping through the cricket world. But he is by no means the only cricketer who misbehaves.

It is only an impression but I believe that Botham becomes even larger than life in the West Indies than in any other part of the world. In my opinion it has to do with his close friendship with Viv Richards. Botham may feel that some of the hero worship accorded to Viv in the Caribbean should, as of right, be his also – he seems to go there with slight feelings of insecurity. Not only that, he is exactly the type of cricketer the West Indians love so maybe he feels this adulation should be his as a right although he is an Englishman. Whatever the reason is I am sure that he competes personally with Viv Richards on the cricket field in the Caribbean. It is interesting, nevertheless, that a cricketer with Botham's record should never have produced his best against the West Indians. There are those who proclaim that Botham is not the player he is built up to be and that he has no answer to the fast bowlers and, indeed, the batsmen when he, himself, is the bowler. I do not go along with this for Botham at his prime was incomparable. But why has he not succeeded against the West Indians as he has done against all other cricketing countries?

There is no clearcut answer to this. I believe that, when Botham played against the West Indies, he tried too hard; he wanted to succeed too much. He did not play against them until 1980, in England, when he had just succeeded Mike Brearley to the captaincy. Botham did not, personally, have much success in a series England lost 1–0 – by no means a disastrous result. But his own failures made him doubly determined to put the record straight in the Caribbean on the 1980–81 tour. By 1984 he had lost the captaincy and, although he did not have a bad series as we have seen, he did not mete out the punishment he had, for example, given to the Australians in 1981. Every time he has played for England against the West Indies he has been increasingly under strong personal pressure. There is then the 'Viv Richards factor' which has, I strongly believe, contributed to his failure both in the Caribbean and against the West Indians in England.

Botham has played so much cricket for Somerset with Richards, he has identified so strongly with him, that when they are on the field, albeit on opposite sides, Botham feels that it is beholden upon him to perform in a comparable manner. I felt this most strongly on Gower's tour of the West Indies in 1985–86. Whenever Botham came in to bat in a Test Match he always seemed to make a point of having an obvious joke with Viv who was captaining the West Indies. He would turn to the slips and say something and laugh. Richards's response, if there was one, was less obvious or noticeable. Botham was not playing to the crowd or to Richards, but more to his own ego. When Richards came in to bat Botham often said something although Richards's response was calm. Richards came in to make runs for the West Indies and let nothing disturb him. Botham, I believe, allowed Richards's prowess as a cricketer to upset him into competing in a rather strange and ineffectual way – for they are not, strictly speaking, comparable cricketers. I have not the slightest doubt that Botham would not agree with this, but then these situations are often the brain-child of the subconscious and how many of us understand our subconscious?

The first 'story' of Gower's tour, however, had nothing whatever to do with Botham. A Fleet Street tabloid dredged up the tale that one of the players was having an affair with the wife of another player who had only just been married. There were other implications and, mercifully, it was never printed which is why I shall name neither player. It was, incidentally, a monstrous yarn which would have stretched even the most energetic of imaginations. David Gower provided us with another foretaste of what was to come in the swimming incident with an air hostess mentioned earlier. There was a mass of hungry eyes all around him and the hostess duly revealed all in a tabloid.

There was a third 'starter' when Ian Wooldridge claimed in the *Daily Mail* that Gooch and Botham were on their final tours for England. Botham was alleged to have told his father-in-law that Lord's was fed up with him and did not want him to go on playing for England. (This was in early 1986.) This is not, in itself, an earth-shattering revelation but it certainly caused unhappiness among the players and much whispering in the corridors of the hotel.

Then we got down to it in earnest. There came the news that the police in Devon and Cornwall had received a dossier believed to have come from a newspaper in London, the same newspaper that Botham was suing for printing allegations that he smoked pot on England's tour of New Zealand two years before. The police had said that they were looking into allegations concerning the misuse of drugs on Botham's recent walk from John O'Groats to Lands End when he had raised nearly £1,000,000 for the Leukaemia Research Fund. Botham's paranoid mistrust of the press was refuelled by this story and caused him, in Port of Spain at any rate, to lead an almost monastic existence in his hotel room away from the prying eyes of telescopic lenses and the scrutiny of Fleet Street. This particular story was, I suppose, simply the rerun of an on-going and long-going saga.

This was quickly followed by the next incident, mentioned earlier, which came from Hollywood. Botham's former agent, Tim Hudson, who was trying to turn Botham into a modern-day Errol Flynn, was alleged to have blown his mouth off at a party in Malibu. Apparently, when asked by a journalist (whose identity he may, or may not, have realized), he said that of course Botham smoked pot and that everyone smoked pot and what of it. That speech occupied the entire front page of one English newspaper and instantly prompted Botham to make a rather public telephone call to Hudson when he was in Miami on his way to Port of Spain. Botham called Hudson from the press-box at the Queen's Park Oval and, by all accounts, spoke fast, loud and furiously to his agent who promptly changed his plans and flew to England. Botham had not minced his words. On arrival at Gatwick Hudson spoke dark words about issuing writs for libel and rushed into the arms of his lawyers. With disarming modesty he said, sometime later, that Botham needed him badly, or words to that effect.

By the time Hudson arrived in London, Botham had made up his mind to sack him and so his much-publicized plans to forge a career in Hollywood vanished overnight. Those plans, in any event, had got no further than a visit to Hollywood before the West Indies tour in which Botham was taken around the studios like some extra and, I daresay, the doyens of Hollywood were none too impressed.

But all of this was no more than a mild skirmish compared with what was to come. The already large contingent of English cricketing journalists on the tour swelled almost daily as newsmen turned up from Fleet Street, their eyes only on Botham. It was the *News of the World* which dropped the bomb when, suddenly, it devoted its first five pages to an exclusive exposure of a sex-and-drug scandal with Botham playing a leading role. A former Miss Barbados, marginally less comely, I gather, than the photographs taken a few years earlier suggested, revealed all the juicy details about a cocaine-snorting frolic and a sex romp. We were told it had all happened in Mick Jagger's house during the Third Test Match in Barbados when the coke had been snorted off the bathroom tiles. There were lively details of an extravagant love-making session in Botham's hotel room during which the bed broke. Botham's performance was also very highly rated which would have pleased him. By that time the lady herself was walled up in a West End hotel in London where she was presumably contemplating, with a less than admirable satisfaction, the not inconsiderable figures on a cheque.

After that little lot the lawyers were quick to get involved. Writs and injunctions were soon flying here, there and everywhere; these, at least, temporarily silenced the *News of the World*. Botham, of course, denied everything whenever he was asked but the fact of it was that, no sooner did he appear a yard outside his hotel bedroom or the dressing-room, than he was besieged by members of the media wanting to know more, wanting quotes on this and quotes on that. It could hardly have been more unsettling, not only for the team who, as we have seen, were up against an extraordinarily powerful force in the West Indies cricket side, but also their main all-rounder, the one man perhaps with a hope of taking the battle to the West Indies and succeeding, was also left in a position in which cricket was at the back of his mind. In any event Botham had come to the West Indies with his attention already distracted from the job of playing cricket by, as we have seen, the lure of gold in Hollywood. It was small wonder that he did not make any significant contributions for England during that series.

By now the tour was in a turmoil and not helped by the business in Port of Spain about Gooch and Antigua. Donald Carr, the Secretary of the Test and County Cricket Board, flew out from England to have long, meaningful discussions with Gooch and, very probably, other members of the team. In the end, as discussed earlier, it was decided that Gooch would go to Antigua for the last Test Match of this ill-fated series. I could not help but feel that, by then, the authorities were obeying the first rule of show-biz which is simply that the show must go on and, of course, on it went. But it stumbled and lurched from crisis to crisis until it entered the realms of soap opera. Only one thing was certain and that was that the lawyers would make a small fortune. The final irony concerning Botham came from the columns of the newspaper which employs him. It said that his wife, Kathy, had made it clear that her husband would never be in trouble in the future for she did not intend to allow him to tour again on his own. Even that statement was to rebound on the Botham family.

All this was quite enough to be going on with from one man and, of course, it kept the media highly involved. The next surprise was to come early the following season (1986) in England on the front page of the *Mail on Sunday*, the paper which had broken the story about Botham and others taking drugs on the 1983–84 tour of New Zealand and Pakistan. That original story had appeared early in 1984, Botham had sued and nothing much seemed to have happened since. Now, Botham admitted that, in spite of all his previous denials, he had – on one or two occasions – smoked pot just as something to try at a party. It was hardly the confession of an addict although I daresay that that front page sold many copies of that particular *Mail on Sunday*. It was hardly a confession either which warranted a nine-week suspension from Test and county cricket – unless a few people knew rather more than the story in the *Mail on Sunday*. Who knows?

— 4 —
The Next in Line

England's selectors make Gower captain *pro tem* • a pugnacious
character in Gatting takes over • Edmonds' and Brearley's
known antagonism • Gatting's captaincy assessed • New
Zealand's debt to Hadlee • his Indian counterpart, Sunil
Gavaskar • both touring sides too good for England.

David Gower was appointed to captain England for the First Test Match
against India in the English summer of 1986; he was given the job for only
one match and was publicly exhorted by Peter May to adopt a more
positive style of leadership. England survived with a draw. Opponents of
the captain found evidence to support their complaints while his backers
were also able to point to incidents which seemed to show that the charges
levelled at him during the winter had hit home. He was selected again for
the Lord's Test in which England were soundly beaten and, at the end of
the match, Gower was sacked and replaced by Mike Gatting. As England
lurched to defeat Gower will have been more aware than anyone of the
inevitable consequence and yet he became even more listless and casual in
appearance. In truth, England were outplayed and, when that happens,
there is not a great deal a captain can do about it. If England had won,
Gower would have survived although his captaincy might have played no
part in the victory. This is further incontrovertible evidence that, if a
captain wants to stay in his job, the only way to guarantee it is to keep on
winning.

Selectors are permanent Aunt Sallys. Whenever anything goes wrong
everything is thrown at them. When their side wins it is the players and
not the selectors who are applauded. It is a thankless task. Having said
this, they do at times, as we shall see much later, make it uncommonly hard
for themselves. Their handling of Gower at the end was as extraordinary as it
was thoughtless. It is natural that, when bodies of men in authority are
criticized, they dig their heels in, obstinately determined to prove themselves
right. It is never easy for anyone to admit error. Gower had seen his side
overwhelmed twice by the West Indies in his short tenure of office but, as we
have seen, there was nothing in the least surprising about that. Mike Brearley
would not have stopped either defeat and it is an interesting point that
Brearley never captained England against the West Indies.

Brearley succeeded Tony Greig in 1977. This was the Australian summer after Kerry Packer's plans to form World Series Cricket had been made public. Greig, an integral part of these plans, was kept in the England side as a player for the Australian series but lost the captaincy. England had played the West Indies in 1976 and another West Indian series was not scheduled until 1980, by which time Brearley had retired from the captaincy. When he was brought back after two Test Matches in 1981 it was for another Australian series. Maybe if it had been the West Indies and not Australia who had toured England in 1977, the story of Brearley's captaincy might have been different.

In between his two West Indian defeats Gower had presided over sides which had beaten India on the sub-continent, never an easy task, and another which had humiliated Australia in England. His record was not that bad and yet, by the time the side returned from the West Indies, the cry for his replacement was strong. With the advantage of hindsight that second defeat was made to seem worse than it was because it followed such a successful series against Australia. England had left for the West Indies after Christmas in 1985 with such high hopes. When hopes are dashed as they were then, the need for someone to blame, the need for a scapegoat, becomes even more urgent, sometimes to the point that it reaches an obsession. Objectivity disappears, as usually happens when everyone starts to leap onto a bandwagon.

It is worth repeating here that Gower was far and away England's most successful batsman in that series in the Caribbean. On his return his every move as captain of Leicestershire was scrutinized, his every utterance dissected and, when he bent down to tie up his boot-laces, observers watched to see if he did it with a purpose that suggested qualities of leadership which had not been previously visible.

Gower had captained England in twenty-three Test Matches by the end of the West Indian tour. The selectors knew by now what sort of captain he was. They should either have dropped him at the start of the 1986 summer or have had a long talk to him and appointed him, at least, for the three-match series against India – New Zealand played three matches in the second half of the summer. Surely, Peter May could have quietly explained the situation to Gower and helped him to do the job without ensuring that the public spotlight was fixed so glaringly upon him. In effect, the selectors suddenly put a pair of 'L' plates on the back of the man they had already entrusted with the job for two years. It was all so unfair on Gower and was yet another of the strange and harmful decisions that have been made over England captains in the last few years. It seems that the selectors had been panicked into feeling that they must do something without having the slightest idea of what to do next.

Times were nothing if not difficult, therefore, when the chunky, bearded, British bull-dog figure of Mike Gatting, who had succeeded

Brearley at Middlesex in 1983, led England out in the Third Test Match against India. A draw was the best he could manage and India, the better side, won the series. It was now New Zealand's turn and, at Trent Bridge, they handed England, who looked much as they had done under Gower, another defeat and we all trooped off to the Oval for the last Test of the summer. By then, Botham had served his sentence, or had had his fishing holiday, and, after a lively knock or two with Somerset, was back in the England side. The crowds were as pleased as the headline writers and the great man failed none of them. With his first ball back in Test cricket he had the New Zealand opener, Bruce Edgar, caught at slip. There were some spectacular blows with the bat although England could only draw the match and so lost another series; but Botham's return had started a buzz in English cricket and the selectors surely had to pick him for the tour of Australia. This would help make up for the absence of Graham Gooch who, after his unhappy tour of the West Indies, had decided to remain at home.

Mike Gatting has always had support in important places which, more than anything, stemmed from the fact that he has played cricket for Middlesex. If you play at Lord's day in and day out it is easier to be noticed, to gain and then retain affection. Gatting is an admirable character, the sort of chap whom everyone who has fought in a trench would like to have beside him. He is an uncomplicated man whose thick-set, determined, thrust-out jaw tells the story. You get what you see.

Gatting had played most of his cricket under Brearley and when Phil Edmonds's determination to be different, if not difficult, had locked him into an unholy confrontation with Brearley which put him out of the running as a likely successor to the Middlesex job and John Emburey's South African excursion had a similar effect, Gatting became the choice. He had Brearley's blessing and, under him, a side which contained at least ten who had played Test cricket; so he continued to win trophies for Middlesex.

At first he was only able to cling precariously to his place in the England side for his technique has always been a worry. He is not the straightest of players and when, in the Lord's Test Match against the West Indies in 1984, he was LBW in both innings to Malcolm Marshall playing no-stroke, it looked as if his Test career might be in for a considerable pause. He continued to score heavily in county cricket, however, and the selectors decided to take him to India that winter where he not only established himself as an England batsman but also became a most important aid to Gower.

Gatting's good form continued against Australia in 1985 and he was one of England's main hopes in the Caribbean the following winter; he was, however, felled by Marshall in that first one-day international in Kingston and returned to England for plastic surgery. His presence was missed badly, as an example, both on and off the field. If Gatting had not been injured it is just possible that that tour would not have been quite so disastrous and that Gower might have held on to the captaincy. Gatting is a tough character and he might have had rather greater success than Gower in coping with the effects of the problems thrown up by Ian Botham. When Gatting returned towards the end of the tour with a new bridge to his nose, his guts and determination were a most welcome addition to a beleaguered side. Once the selectors had taken the decision to replace Gower, Gatting was the only possible successor, although he should never have been more than a number two.

As we have seen, Gatting's chance to captain Middlesex and then England was helped enormously by the on-going feud between Brearley and Edmonds. Both were at public schools, both captained Cambridge and both are extremely intelligent. When Edmonds joined Middlesex it seemed reasonable, from every point of view, to suppose that he would inherit the captaincy at Lord's and that he might also, a few years later, become a logical successor to the England captaincy. But something went wrong. Whether it was a personality clash, a dislike built out of one incident or simply, as I suspect, Edmonds's studied determination to be eccentric and different, he and Brearley did not like each other. Edmonds did not respect Brearley's much-publicized intellect, saying as much whenever he could and endlessly goading his captain. Edmonds must have enjoyed waging the battle or surely he would have joined another county – many would have had him.

In the end, it cost Edmonds more than Brearley, who would have regarded Edmonds as a nuisance without allowing too much emotional involvement to come into it. Brearley captained Middlesex and England with enormous success and was one of the game's great captains. Edmonds, on the other hand, left the game after the 1987 season as an enigma with a talent which was never much more than three-quarters fulfilled, principally because of a perverse attitude to life which could, perhaps, be called colossal arrogance. He was a good cricketer but, with such a great natural talent, he should have achieved much more. To listen to Edmonds justifying his reasons for bowling badly or for deliberately ignoring a not inconsiderable batting ability is to understand why he drove his captains to despair. Most of it was questionable logic, to say the least, although, by the end, I am sure he had convinced himself to believe all, or most, of what he said. It was such a sad waste.

History, and not just the history of cricket, has been studded with blood feuds which, to dispassionate viewers, seem infantile and stupid, ever since Cain and Abel got up to their tricks. Brearley and Edmonds was one such example, although not one likely to have such far-reaching consequences. Why should two such intelligent men have allowed a situation like this to start, let alone develop to the point where it got so out of hand? How could two able intellects be so stupid? How could Brearley, whom the Australian fast bowler, Rodney Hogg, described so adroitly as having a degree in people and who is now a considerable psychoanalyst, have allowed it to continue? What was Edmonds trying to gain from it all? Could they not see the side-effects? Was there no one who could have banged their heads together? Where were the Middlesex committee or even the England selectors in all of this? Why did Edmonds need to try to put Brearley down? What was he trying to prove? He will give an answer in his own way, one less inconsequential than it sounds, and, when he is finished, will probably be the most likely person to believe all that he has said.

Edmonds has now left Middlesex after deciding only to continue playing for them under terms of his own which were patently unacceptable even to a committee which has done double-somersaults to accommodate him. He wanted to play without being paid and, therefore, without being subject to any discipline even the 'optional practice' of the West Indian tour. Of course, Edmonds will argue to the death that those who have turned him away are stupid to ignore such an offer. He is an inflexible chap who sees only black and white; who revels in his own contrariness; who is, and always will be, a most stimulating companion with a string of vibrant ideas, some good, some crazy, all put forward with great certainty.

Edmonds has now gone off to the Golden Mile to try and make squillions. Maybe he will succeed in rocking the foundations of the City of London. You may be sure, though, that he, like his splendid wife, will always be highly entertaining. I would welcome Phil Edmonds and Mrs Phil Edmonds at any dinner party I ever gave; I'm not so sure that I would want Mr Edmonds in my cricket side.

Not the least of Gatting's problems, both with Middlesex and England, has been to try to control and utilize the talents of Edmonds. Probably because he finds it irresistible, or maybe because old habits die hard, Edmonds has goaded, taunted and tested Gatting too; he will have his usual, rational, little-boy-lost explanations for each incident. In 1986 Gatting was unable to save the series against India and went on to lose to New Zealand and, in both series, England undoubtedly lost to the better side.

In those four Tests in 1986 Gatting showed himself to be a stereotyped thinker about the game. Neither his bowling changes nor his field placings showed any real imagination and, during his tenure of office, one has several times seen him at loggerheads, especially with his spin bowlers, over field placings. His battles with Edmonds have probably been inevitable but he has had words, also, with John Emburey, an altogether different, more modest and outwardly unassuming character. At this level of the game I would have thought that a captain must, except in very exceptional circumstances, allow a bowler to have the field he wants. Gatting's refusal to do so pinpoints an obstinacy in his character which has not always been an asset and which was to let him down later in Pakistan. He may be a thoroughly worthy chap but this does not necessarily make him a good captain. His one piece of luck, since taking over the England captaincy, was to have Micky Stewart as his cricket manager in Australia in 1986–87. Gatting allowed Stewart to take over many of the captain's duties and they worked well together – to start with at any rate. Theirs was a relationship which comes into focus in a later chapter when we look at England in Australia.

As we have seen, he made little impression on India and New Zealand in his first attempts at leading the England side. These two series underline one of the more interesting aspects of international cricket in recent years. At this time of West Indian domination there has been a significant improvement in the fortunes of India, New Zealand and Pakistan who once used to be the easy pickings of Test cricket. The recent rise of each country has had a great deal to do with the ability of three extraordinary players.

We will see later how Imran Khan has towered over Pakistan cricket in a way that few individuals have ever dominated one side. New Zealand's excellent run, which looks as if it may have ended for the time being largely because of old age, owed most to the fast bowling of Richard Hadlee; while much of India's success has been attributable to the astonishing batting powers of their opener Sunil Gavaskar.

Richard Hadlee lends substance to the truism about bowlers winning matches. New Zealand's remarkable run of success in the 1980s has revolved almost entirely around his quite brilliant fast bowling. Hadlee typifies the hard-nosed professional in the post-Packer era. He has become, arguably, the best fast-medium seam bowler the game has ever known. At the start of the eighties he decided that, if he was to keep going into cricketing old age, he must cut down his run and stop life as a tearaway fast bowler. Off no more than a dozen paces his control, as he moves the ball into and away from the bat, is extraordinary, as is his pace. In the 1987–88 series in Australia, Craig McDermott ran in twice as far and did not find the same speed. Hadlee, with his mechanism finely tuned like a Formula One car, has as fluent and irresistible a run- up as I have seen. Bowling from close to the stumps he has a well-nigh perfect action. I was lucky enough to see him take sixteen wickets against Australia in the First Test in Brisbane in 1985–86 but he was scarcely less impressive two years later and I shall never forget the manner in which he tormented and destroyed Dean Jones in the three Test Matches in Australia in 1987–88. It is a comment both on one-day cricket and on the batting of Jones that, in the subsequent one-day internationals when there is seldom more than one slip and one gulley at a time, he got away with it. Somehow it is a bad joke that a bowler of Hadlee's skills should ever be asked to take part in a one-day defensive operation with such an insulting field.

Hadlee played a considerable part in New Zealand's victories in England and in his lovely, lithe, left-handed way, he is a wonderful straight hitter of the ball, especially against the fast bowlers. He is another player who has the talent to have made more runs than he has, but, as a bowler, he has had to do it single-handedly for New Zealand. At the other end he has mostly had the good and faithful Euen Chatfield who has been a sterling partner but has not been able to soften up the batsmen as another fast bowler would have done. Hadlee and Chatfield were never a Trueman and Statham or a Lillee and Thomson.

I appear, from the above, to have chosen Hadlee ahead of Lillee. As a fast-medium bowler off a short run I think this is the case; as a genuine fast bowler, most certainly not. Lillee cut down his run later in his career when he developed that famous leg cutter. He was still a fine bowler although he never quite matched Hadlee in this form. As an out-and-out fast bowler Hadlee would never have claimed to have been Lillee's equal. In 1974–75 and, again, in 1975–76 when Australia destroyed first England and then the West Indies, the majesty of Dennis Lillee was awe-inspiring – his run-up, his action and then that ferocious appeal at the end of it all. At the other end, Jeff Thomson looked more like a primaeval force than a fast bowler and the combination was devastating.

I have earlier described Hadlee as a thoroughly modern professional. Seam and swing bowling have been his life and he has approached the job with a dedication that even Geoffrey Boycott would have admired. He is supremely fit with not a spare ounce of flesh. A man of relatively few words, Hadlee goes about his business behind that black moustache with an inscrutable singleness of purpose and an expression which is sometimes not far away from a scowl. He knows exactly how he is going to bowl to each batsman and he leaves nothing to chance. I daresay he lives his life the same way.

I was lucky enough to share a Television New Zealand commentary box with him during England's series in New Zealand in 1987–88. His comments were as clinical and as pointed as his bowling and he was always well worth listening to. He has a nice, quiet, if slightly shy, sense of humour and, occasionally, comes out with a ripe one-liner. There is a natural modesty about him too. His life is dedicated to taking wickets and in doing this he narrows the margin for error as much as he can. Hadlee may not be a natural companion for an evening out with Ian Botham but he would always be a bowler I would want to have on my side. If Hadlee had been taken out of New Zealand cricket this last decade they would not have won very much. Supporters of Martin Crowe may raise an eyebrow or two here but, as I have said, it has always been bowlers who win Test Matches. It would have been nice to have chosen another fast bowling all-rounder, Kapil Dev, as the principal ingredient in India's success over the last few years, and he has undoubtedly had a big part to play. Like Ian Botham he has gone somewhat off the boil in the last year or two, however, and I feel that India has owed most to Sunil Gavaskar. This may seem to fly in the face of my statement, made above, about bowlers winning matches. Gavaskar is an exception to this. In his Test career, which stretched from 1970 to 1987, Gavaskar scored thirty-four centuries in 125 Test matches, five more than Don Bradman who played in only fifty-two Test matches – another example of how far ahead Bradman was of anyone else.

In his first ever Test series Gavaskar enabled India to beat the West Indies in 1970–71 in the Caribbean when, in four Test Matches, he scored 774 runs. In 1975 at Lord's in India's first ever World Cup match, however, he batted 60 overs for 36 runs and made certain that, whatever slight chance India had of beating England, disappeared. This was the perverse side of his character or maybe he had not been told that you cannot draw a one-day match; the whole idea was very new in those days. At the Oval in 1979 he made 221 in the fourth innings against England when India needed 438 to win. They failed by 9 runs with two wickets left after Gavaskar had almost won another match with the bat in one of the greatest innings ever played. There are many other examples of the man's genius over the years.

Early in his career Gavaskar was a stodgy performer with a proud and impeccable defensive technique and an unending supply of concentration. As the years went by, he learned new tricks and, by the time his career ended, he had become a wonderfully exciting and controlled hitter at the start of an innings. Maybe opening the batting with Srikkanth had rubbed off on him and, having once swung the bat and connected, he found that he liked life in the fast lane. By the end he was almost addicted. I shall never forget the innings he played in the 1987 World Cup against Australia and New Zealand about which I have written at greater length later in the book. He combined technique – no one has played straighter – flair and footwork with the considerable wicket-craft he accumulated as his career went on.

Gavaskar is small with eyes that twinkle like his footwork. He has a lovely sense of humour which he did not introduce into his batting until his impish period towards the end. Earlier, he was a solid, almost statuesque figure at the crease; later, he advanced down the pitch and, grinning under that home-made plaster of Paris crash helmet, would straight drive a fast bowler for 6 in the very first over of the innings. Gavaskar thought deeply about the game and should have captained India more than he did. Like Imran, he suffered from the sub-continental habit of changing captains when a series is lost. It was sad for Indian cricket that he and Kapil Dev should not have hit it off too well together. This never reached the Brearley/Edmonds level but Kapil and Gavaskar saw the game differently, just as their life styles were different.

Kapil Dev took reckless chances; Gavaskar, who reserved his riskiest feats of hitting for one-day cricket, did not. Gavaskar would have been better at giving advice to younger players. Kapil Dev lived and played by instinct and did not always bother to analyse. In spite of his formidable record I doubt that India got the best out of Gavaskar. I spoke to him in Delhi during the World Cup in 1987; we were talking about comparing Test cricket and one-day cricket and he gave me a marvellous example of his sense of humour. He quite clearly preferred the longer drawn-out form of the game to the instant one-day cricket, yet he said, 'I hope when I have retired that another Test Match is never played, for that will mean no one will ever beat my record of scoring 10,000 runs in Test cricket.' He gave a big chuckle and his shoulders heaved.

Gavaskar and Hadlee have been two great men of cricket, two players worth the journey and the gate money alone. They have had a remarkable impact on the contemporary game. Imran is the third. These are players who have done well out of the game and who will, I am sure, in their different ways, put back a great deal into cricket in their respective countries. All of us who love cricket have been enriched by a command performance by any one of them. Above all, they have been supreme patriots and their prime concern has been to lift their countries in the world rankings and, in this, each one has been gratifyingly and absorbingly successful. Of course, there have been others but this tribute is not about them.

In 1986 Gavaskar and Hadlee were two of the main problems confronting Gatting in his first outing as England's captain, not least because players such as these have a habit of causing their colleagues to play above their usual standard. If Gatting was to be successful in upsetting India in the Third and last Test Match, or New Zealand in the following three-match series, he would have needed either a lot of luck or a flash or two of inspiration; but Gatting never suggested he was going to be another Mike Brearley. It was soon apparent that he was a limited thinker about the game. Maybe he gave the impression of taking a more positive role than Gower, but there was nothing over-imaginative about the way he ran the game.

Gatting was another captain who, rather than try to make things happen, waited in the hope that something would turn up. He never looked like getting more out of his players against India and New Zealand than Gower had done, although his supporters would say that the tempo of the summer had been set by Gower's apparent lethargy. I am not sure. I also gained the impression that Gatting is as obstinate and inflexible in some of his views as his jawline suggests. By the end of 1986 it was a formality that Gatting should have been appointed to take the side to

Australia. Whether anyone thought that England had acquired a better captain than Gower I rather doubt.

Peter May was always the enigmatic figure in these captaincy changes. Having kicked out Keith Fletcher the moment he took the job on as chairman, he appointed Bob Willis to whom he showed deep loyalty. Popular demand, as we have seen, pleaded Gower's case and he took over from Willis. Then came the extraordinary affair of Gower being appointed for the First and then the Second Test Match against India in 1986. This was followed by the sack. Gatting could do nothing about India and New Zealand, but he led England to victory in Australia and was then beaten by Pakistan in England. The World Cup and the tour of Pakistan followed, and Gatting had his disgraceful run-in with umpire Shakoor Rana. He was desperately lucky that it did not cost him the captaincy. He then decided to tell the full story in an autobiography which might have cost him his job, but by then he was the centrepiece of a sex scandal which did. During the First Test against the West Indies at Trent Bridge Gatting was named as one of the principals in a late-night sex romp at the team's hotel. A waitress from a neighbouring restaurant told of her torrid love scenes with the England captain. The selectors met at Lord's on the Thursday. Gatting was called and at the end of it all Peter May read a statement which said that, while the selectors believed all that Gatting had told them and that he had not made love to the girl, they had withdrawn their invitation to captain England in the Second Test, because he had acted irresponsibly taking a lady to his room late at night. The next day John Emburey was named as England's captain for the Second Test at Lord's. This is, of course, going miles ahead of the story, but the question remains: was Gatting a victim of selectorial prudishness or of his own arrogance? In chapter 15 we will have a closer look.

— 5 —
Oddjob at the Astrodome

October 1986: baseball at the Houston Astrodome • showbiz
colour and atmosphere • parallelled by Kerry Packer's World
Series cricket • comparisons between the two games • the art
of pitching • the umpire brooks no interference • cricket
packaged in such a setting.

I travelled to Australia in October 1986 by way of Houston where I was
lucky enough to see, for the first time, a top-class game of baseball. I must
say straight away that I found it one of the most exciting experiences of my
sporting life. On the drive from the airport to the city my friend, who had
been racking her brains trying to think of things to do with me for five
days, told me that she had managed to get hold of two tickets for the
second match in the best-of-seven the Astros were playing against the
New York Mets at the Astrodome in the finals of the National League
Championship series.

I found the Astrodome easily the most exciting part of Houston and I
shall never forget my first visit. As we drove there I felt like a little boy
who was going to the Big Top for the first time to see a circus. We could
see the huge dome of the stadium for some distance before we arrived and
I could not wait to get inside. I was terrified that we would spend an age
getting into the car park and miss all the preliminaries and the first few
minutes of the game. I need not have worried. The car park was the most
easily accessible I have ever seen for any big sporting occasion. We turned
right into the park about twenty-five minutes before the start and were in
our seats along with about 45,000 others precisely seven minutes later.

I have always wondered why cricket and baseball should, apparently,
be mutually exclusive and why the two games could not happily coexist.
Were they really as far apart as the Atlantic Ocean? Was cricket a dated,
dyed-in-the-wool British colonial pastime which belonged to a bygone
age and had no place in the fast-moving US of A? Was it one big, boring
yawn which would send all self-respecting Americans to sleep? And was
baseball so dynamic, so full of excitement, so stuffed to the eyeballs with
hype and showbiz razzamatazz as to make cricket a distant country
cousin with straw sticking out of its hair? Would American crowds turn
their noses up even at an instantly digestible form of the good old English

game? These were some of the things I wanted to find the answer to as well, of course, as trying to discover what baseball was all about.

After climbing the concrete stairs at breakneck speed we walked through the tunnel-like entrance to the stand. As we came out of the shadow into the brilliant glare of the floodlights it was as if the whole Astrodome was erupting all around and over us, just like one of those super fireworks which go whistling high into the night, leaving everyone in suspense, before bursting into irresistible umbrellas of coloured stars. For a moment I did not know where to look as I shuffled, mesmerized, to my seat.

It was too much to take in at once as I stumbled down the steps, looking everywhere except where I was going. It was an exhilarating kaleidoscope of colour and noise which swept over us in bigger and ever more deafening waves. The enormous banks of floodlights helped give an atmosphere straight from the realms of fiction. The huge electronic scoreboard, amply fed by its computers, was providing fact upon fact about the participants in glorious technicolour on the replay screen. The six-tiered stands rose high into the sky, thumping music blared out insistently, acres of dark green astroturf gleamed invitingly, players in their coloured strips were practising down below us, a partisan crowd was already warming to its work, red paper cups full to the brim with popcorn were being carried to and fro by the patrons, packets of monkey nuts and beer were also in heavy demand and, believe it or not, there was a roof on top of it all.

We were sitting in excellent seats almost directly behind, and some distance above, the striker. Baseball is played in a right angle, bisected by the striker and the pitcher, and, when hit, the ball has to stay inside this right angle. The hum of excitement all through the stadium was produced by a dramatic local sense of expectancy for, on the previous night, the local lads, the Astros, had caused quite an upset, putting it across their New York rivals (the hot favourites to win) by 1–0. There is nothing a sporting crowd loves more than an upset of this sort, especially if you support the underdogs. Could it happen again?

You will see from all this why, by the time the Astros pitcher, Nolan Ryan, began to wind himself up for the first pitch of the night, I felt that cricket had a difficult job living up to this. Having spent forty-five minutes earlier in the day waiting at a level crossing while the second longest goods train in the world rattled slowly past, drawn by no less than four huge diesel engines, I already felt that Houston was nothing if not a city of contrasts.

Of course, I did not understand the finer parts of the game and I am sure that I missed most of them altogether but, in no time at all, I was on the edge of my seat, living each moment as the roars of approval or the groans of disappointment, greeting every deed performed below us, acted as my emotional compass. The competition was sharp and soon a fierce verbal battle was being fought between the players. This sledging made anything that happens at the Sydney Cricket Ground, when the batsman is surrounded by close fielders, look faint-hearted in the extreme.

The proceedings were presided over by a huge uncompromising umpire, dressed in black, whom I immediately and irreverently christened Oddjob after Ian Fleming's splendid character in one of the James Bond novels. Once, after Oddjob had made a decision, two chaps ran onto the pitch and argued and gesticulated wildly but, of course, to no effect. They were the two managers and brave fellows they were, too, for I would never in a million years have dared to dispute Oddjob's word. It all helped the excitement.

Sledging – calling your opponent every name you can think of – is an accepted part of baseball and no one gets too squeamish about it. I enjoyed enormously a paragraph in that morning's paper about the previous day's game. It read:

> It was, in fact, those practitioners of winning by intimidation [the Mets] who looked a bit weak in the knees against Mike Scott [the Astros' pitcher]. In the words of Dave Smith who wasn't needed, 'I don't know of any team that wouldn't have been intimidated by him tonight.' The irridescent symbol of New York frustration wore a big '8' on his back. Gary Carter, odds-on favorite to win National League most-valuable-player honors, club spokesman and one of the few men alive who could provoke Scott to verbal sparring, wasn't even most-valuable bitcher.

Play had been underway for about twenty minutes when the light dawned. What I was looking at was the birth of Kerry Packer's World Series Cricket ten years on. It was all there in front of me. The visionary, back in the mid-seventies (whether Packer himself or one of his television brains-trust), had seen, in an increasingly Americanized Australian society, the appeal of an instant, easily digestible form of cricket. One-day cricket was there for the taking and all that was needed was to dress it up, actually and figuratively, with the full showbiz treatment and the turnstiles would never stop. And so it has proved.

Having tumbled to this, it may have helped me answer some of the questions I posed earlier in the chapter. Limited-over cricket and baseball, thanks to lashings of hype, have plenty in common. The Astrodome would be a perfect place to stage a forty-over cricket match, for that venue could not help but heighten the anticipation and the drama which has been on view under floodlights at the Sydney Cricket Ground for almost ten years. A partisan crowd is a necessity and, with skilful marketing, could be arranged. In one sense, though, baseball undoubtedly has it over cricket. It is a simpler, less complicated game for the spectator; this makes it easier for those who do not want their excitement cluttered up with a need for specialist knowledge. In any event, why should a nation be turned on by a game which is not all that different from its own national game, especially when it is affected by an element of that nose-in-the-air smugness which seems to be a prerogative of the English? I accept all this, but I still feel that an even sharper, more abbreviated form of limited-over cricket than a forty-over match would have an excitement which would enable it to live on the same stage as baseball. With sensible streamlining and clever marketing – and this latter is surely the most essential ingredient –it would be fun to have a try.

As I watched that evening in Houston I thought that a film of the two games side by side might not be a bad idea. As it is, cricket is far from being unknown in the USA for there are significant numbers of expatriates from cricket-playing countries living there. League cricket flourishes in Florida where many West Indians live; former West Indian off-spinner, Lance Gibbs, is still taking a hatful of wickets there each weekend. Cricket is played in California where it was started in Hollywood by Aubrey Smith who captained England in the 1890s against South Africa. Cricket is, indeed, played anywhere that West Indians, Pakistanis, Indians, Englishmen, and all those brought up in any cricket- playing country, are grouped together. Not long ago there was an idea to build a cricket stadium as part of a huge sporting complex in Florida and to stage home West Indian Test Matches there. That still might be a good thought for it could only help West Indian finances.

While I was completely sucked in by the glamour of the occasion at the Astrodome, this was not a classic contest. The Mets remained solidly, if unglamorously, in charge and gained revenge for their defeat the night before. They won by a 5–1 margin although there were no home runs and it was work-a-day baseball. Because of the importance of the result, though, and the acute partisanship, the crowd was vibrant even if it became subdued in the closing stages as the Mets strengthened their hold. I think I was probably more gripped than my guide who, every now and then, ducked out and returned with fresh supplies of popcorn and beer.

As the evening wore on, I made one discovery which I found staggering. If anything, baseball is a slower game than cricket. If I had been able to time on a stopwatch the moments of direct action in the course of one hour, they would not have added up to as many minutes as the equivalent action in one hour's cricket. I know I shall be accused of being prejudiced but I am sure that this would have been true. In a theatrical sense, it is the full production and the razzamatazz which gives baseball its apparent pace and slickness. It is this which gives one-day international cricket some of its appeal in Australia. Five-day Test Matches will never become part of American life but I can't, for the life of me, see why a shrewdly produced and marketed form of limited-over cricket should not be popular. I have no doubt that a hurricane 50 by Ian

Botham or Viv Richards at the Astrodome would provide continuous excitement and drama which is, as yet, unknown in baseball.

So far, I have talked about the general impressions of the evening. I am certainly not qualified to be critical of the play although some of the technical aspects of the game fascinated me. It seemed to me that the pitcher is the key to the game. He is a most exciting figure as he winds himself up before every ball, pivoting round in the small circle in which he stands as if he is going to throw a discus. He throws the ball about fifteen yards and has to combine speed, accuracy and swing at least as precisely as his counterpart in cricket, the fast bowler. The game began – I never discovered how it was decided that the Mets would strike first – with Nolan Ryan pitching for the Astros and beginning well. But the more interesting of the two pitchers and the man who, to a great extent, controlled the way the game went, was Bob Ojeda for the Mets. He was the smaller of the two, pitched with his left hand, and had a satisfying, lithe and fluent throwing action. It was impossible to see how he gripped the ball but he achieved extraordinary late swing and pinpoint accuracy. He had the ability to make the ball dip late in its flight so that, when it reached the striker, it was only a few inches off the ground and difficult to hit.

Every now and then one of the Astros made contact but the ball seldom went far enough to enable him to scramble round to more than first base. There was one lovely blow which sent the white ball streaking down the stadium where it was caught with ridiculous ease by one of the fielders in that huge glove they wear on their left hand. Time and again, the strikers swung vainly at Ojeda who achieved a succession of strike-outs which come when a striker misses three legal pitches in succession. A tip-top pitcher may earn as much as four million dollars a year; an equivalent fast bowler would do well to earn one fifteenth of that. For all that, the skills do not seem to be that far apart although one bowls and the other throws.

Another intriguing figure is the catcher who squats like cricket's equivalent, the wicket-keeper, close behind the striker; he wears pads, gloves, vizor and, no doubt, several invisibles. Whenever the striker missed or the ball was wide, the catcher invariably took the ball cleanly in his left glove. I thought that this performance alone was worth the entrance money. In the field, too, the standard of fielding and catching was amazingly high. It was very clear that every member of the side was trained, to as near perfection as possible, in the performance of his own individual skills. The coaches and management had left as little as possible to chance. Big money usually leads to increased efficiency and big-time baseball could hardly be more streamlined or professional. The players were superbly fit. The American public rightly demands top performances from its highly paid sports stars and, if they fail to produce, there are plenty more waiting for the chance.

The performer who held my attention more than any other was Oddjob whose position seemed to me to be the most perilous of all. Dressed in black trousers, black blazer and black cap he had a sinister aspect. The umpire stands no more than four or five feet behind the striker in a position which, in cricketing terms, would be a very close first slip. The striker stands at the ready with his bat raised and the pitcher has to throw the ball so that it flies over the main course plate-sized round disc in front of the striker's feet. It is Oddjob's duty to make sure that the ball is not wide and therefore unfair. If it is, he steps smartly forward with his right arm and index finger raised. It seemed to me that Oddjob was in mortal danger, although he wore a white vizor which he took off after every ball and shoved on again as he sat on his haunches to scrutinize the next ball. He would also have had innumerable invisibles to guard those tender spots. His size alone gave one the impression that it would have been most unprofitable to have had a real run-in with him. When, at intervals, the managers of the two teams ran out to argue with him, I could have told them that they were wasting their time, but maybe it was a performance which had to be gone through. Come to think of it, perhaps it would increase the entertainment value of limited-over cricket if the managers were allowed to run out and shout the odds with the umpires. The only flash of colour in Oddjob's otherwise all-black outfit was the number 23 in white which perched on his right sleeve just below the shoulder. When he crouched down and glared ferociously at the pitcher, as he began to wind himself up, one could only fear for the man who dared to err. Oddjob should have had an unpronounceable Eastern European name of at least twenty-eight letters and also been a member of Smersh or Spectre. In fact, as I later discovered, his name, most inappropriately I thought, was simply Doug Harvey. Judging from comments in the papers he is a much respected umpire and probably a kind and genial soul to boot. But he gave the game an extra dimension that night at the Astrodome.

All through the evening I kept looking for, and finding, similarities with cricket; some of these were stranger than others. The most amusing had occured the day before and had been much written about in that morning's papers. Mike Scott, the Astros' pitcher, who had effectively won them the opening game, had, at one stage, been accused by the Mets of doctoring the ball with an illegal substance, presumably in order to make it swing further. The striker had protested. I am sure the manager ran out and had his two bob's worth while the unruffled Oddjob adjudicated. He studied the ball with great care before deciding that it was in mid-season condition but Gary Carter, whom we already know to be a dab hand as a sledger, had his say and the crowd really got after him. Maybe it was all good, clean fun, but it took me back to the Chepauk Stadium in Madras in 1976–77 when England's left-arm fast bowler, John Lever, was accused by the Indians of using Vaseline from his eyebrows to make the ball shine and therefore swing. Nothing was proved but many indignant Indians felt sure that they had a satisfactory alibi for being badly beaten in the first three Test Matches in that series. Back at the Astrodome, Scott got his own back when without mixing words he accused Carter of talking too much. The last word was left to the manager of the Mets, Davey Johnson, who came to Carter's defence with the succinct and immortal remark about Alan Ashby of the Astros. He said, presumably through clenched teeth, 'Alan Ashby ain't no day in the park either.' It was good clean stuff.

The only thing I was sad about that night was that we never saw a home run. The few big hits were not big enough and were mostly caught in the deep. One or two others faded out of the right angle into the crowd and were out of bounds. We left shortly before the end, just after the crowd had started to perform the Mexican Wave. Yes, we had that, too, in Test Matches in England in 1986.

There was, naturally, so much I had not understood and probably a great deal that I had not even noticed, but it was a terrific experience and I can't wait for more. As I left the Astrodome I wondered if an American who was as ignorant about cricket as I was of baseball, before that night, would have come away from his first cricket match with anything like the same feelings of exhilaration. What fun it would be to put it to the test and stage a limited-over cricket match in this fabulous setting. As I have already said, World Series cricket came from the Astrodome and so why don't we take it back there?

By the end of the week I realized, also, that my own trade, cricket reporting and probably commentating, had plenty to learn from those who practise the art at the Astrodome and similar venues around the USA. I shall end this chapter with a few words from Al Carter in the *Houston Chronicle* the morning after the Astros had caused that first remarkable upset by beating the Mets 1–0. These were the first three paragraphs of his piece.

> 'What was that saying? Ya gotta be-leeve!'
> 'Sounds good. Go with it.'
> 'Yeah, man. Ya gotta be-leeve! When the Astros load the bases with one out against Dwight Gooden and the pitcher happens to be the man strolling to the plate and the rally is dead meat, ya gotta be-leeve. And when the same thing happens again two innings later, well, ya gotta be-leeve.'

I couldn't have put it better myself.

Then, I caught an aeroplane to Australia where I was able to check out my comparison with one-day cricket. But first it was the Ashes series, although before even that began I had a train to catch.

— 6 —

A Dusty Eternity

An abject start to the Ashes series 1986–87 • rest and
recuperation in good company across the Nullarbor Plain • a
splendid steward named 'Squizzy' • one of the world's greatest
train rides.

England, with Ian Botham on board and Mike Gatting in charge, set off
for Australia in October 1986 somewhat chastened by events of the
English summer but confident that, for all that, they could repeat their
triumph of 1985 over Australia. Of all the forty-odd tours I have covered,
this one was to make one of the more extraordinary starts. Australia is
always an exhilarating country in which to arrive. I completed the long
haul from Houston by kind permission of Continental Airlines and soon
found myself addressing my first plate of Sydney rock oysters. I think it
was two days after leaving the Astrodome, although I am never quite sure
how it works when crossing the International Dateline in that direction.

Net practice for the England players took place in Brisbane and was
followed by a three-day match against a country eleven in Bundaberg,
best known for its rum. It was a useful flexing-of-the-muscles exercise
and was followed by two one-day games, also against country opponents.
The serious cricket then began in Brisbane with a four-day match against
Queensland at the Gabba; the state demolished England with a day to
spare. It was a most inglorious start and Gatting's side produced some
thoroughly shabby cricket and deserved everything that they got. It was a
result which was of no great significance in itself except that it can only be
bad for morale when a touring side is walloped in its first match.
Individual and collective confidence suffers while it makes the host
country feel pretty smug.

It did no one any harm, not least those people who were trying to sell
the series to the public, that England should now encounter a poor South
Australian side which they beat on the fourth afternoon. If the spinners,
and especially Phil Edmonds, had bowled better it would have been over
earlier. One encouraging aspect of the game was a good hundred from
James Whitaker in his opening first-class innings of the tour. He had been
the one rather surprising choice when the side had been selected, although
he had had a good season for Leicestershire in 1986. Now, he showed why

the selectors had preferred him to Northamptonshire's Robert Bailey and one or two others. Alas, this was to be Whitaker's one brief moment in the sun during the entire tour. He was not chosen to play against Western Australia in the last game before the First Test Match; this decision made it clear that the tour selectors were not going to consider him for the First Test. This was most unlucky for him for it was the only time on the tour when he had some form to build on and, after that, he hardly had a chance although injuries brought him into the side for the Third Test Match.

By the time the South Australian match drew towards its end my mind was concerned only with the importance of an early finish – for some of us had decided to do the next stage of the journey by what must be one of the great railway journeys. The original idea was dreamed up in Brisbane at the start of the tour by Graham Otway who is the cricket correspondent of *Today*. We had to move from Adelaide to Kalgoorlie where, two days after beating South Australia, England were to take on a Western Australian country eleven. The party was scheduled to fly out of Adelaide in the morning and wait for four hours in Perth before flying up to the famous old gold-mining town.

Our plan was to catch the Indian Pacific Express in Adelaide at six o'clock in the evening after the South Australian match had ended. The train would decant us some twenty-eight hours later in Kalgoorlie after rumbling across the Nullarbor Plain. The first recruit had been Peter West who, after retiring from BBC Television at the end of the English summer, had been asked to cover the tour of Australia by the *Daily Telegraph*. In a long and distinguished career, Peter had never travelled with an England cricket side to Australia and, as it was his one remaining ambition, he leapt at the chance. While there he was determined to see as much of the country as the busy timetable of a cricket tour would allow.

Scyld Berry, who labours on behalf of the *Observer*, had made the journey but in the opposite direction on a previous tour; he also decided to come and Peter did not have to work very hard to persuade me to sign up. He and I bought our first-class tickets – we were determined to do it in comfort – for the sum of $303 each which we thought, at the time, was pretty reasonable. As it happened, I think he and I were the only two in our party who actually paid for our tickets. It was at about this time that I asked three of the England players, David Gower, Phil Edmonds and Allan Lamb, to come to dinner one evening. I told them about our intended journey and Gower and Edmonds were on board in no time at all. Lamb is perhaps a little more restless and I could not help but feel that he would be like a caged lion on a twenty-eight hour train journey. He appeared to have similar thoughts. Peter Lush, the England manager, had no objection to Gower and Edmonds coming with us. A late recruit was the well-known cricket photographer, Adrian Murrell; ironically the only casualty was Graham Otway whose newspaper decided it wanted him to go to Melbourne to cover the Melbourne Cup, to be run at the same time. As it happened, his paper withdrew this particular commission at the last moment when it was too late for him to join us.

Although I am probably the only person ever to think so, the Nullarbor Plain seemed to have a romantic ring about it. The name also reminds me of a lovely Australian story. Jim Swanton, the famous cricket writer whose name seldom fails to come up when two or three cricketers are gathered together in any part of the world, made his last working tour to Australia to watch the West Indies in 1975–76. The First Test Match was played in Brisbane and the Second in Perth and, because in the past he had always flown, he now decided to go from Sydney to Perth by train. In those days the train stopped at the borders of each state where the crew was changed so that, in New South Wales, the crew were New South Welshmen, in South Australia they were South Australians and so on. Jim boarded the train one afternoon in Sydney and, at the appropriate hour before dinner, made his way to the bar in the first-class section of the train and, when asked by the barman what he would like to drink, said that he would like a pink gin; this was mixed and administered and very good it was too. The next time Jim came to the bar was sometime before lunch on the following day; by this time the train had moved into South Australia. The barman was now a muscular South Australian who may have had strong views about Poms. He asked Jim what he would like to drink and also received a request for a pink gin. On hearing this he looked hard at Jim and said loudly in a broad ocker voice, 'Mate, we only carry white fuckin' gin on this ship.'

We faced only one problem which was logistical. If England and South Australia battled it out right to the bitter end the game would not finish until at least six o'clock, the time the train was to depart. Mercifully, England made short work of the state side, our contingency plans did not have to be put into action and Peter West and I arrived at the brand new Keswick Station in Adelaide with plenty of time to spare.

As we talked in the bar the train, which had come from Sydney through Broken Hill, pulled into the station and at about the same time a taxi produced Gower, Edmonds, Berry and Murrell – so we had a full complement. We were also joined by the manager of the Australian National Railways who told us that a special coach with six single cabins was going to be added to the train in Adelaide. He said, too, that he had arranged for all drinks at meal times to be on the house and I wondered if he had any idea of what he was letting himself in for. We were, the cricketers excepted of course, a reasonably thirsty bunch.

After a good deal of shunting and clanging our special coach was put on to the train, next door to the restaurant car, and the great moment arrived when we stepped onto the platform to take possession of it. Our bags had already been carried on board and, although it was well past six o'clock, no one was in any hurry for the train to start. We were introduced to the splendid steward who would look after us all the way to Kalgoorlie. He answered to the name of 'Squizzy' Taylor; all Taylors in Australia are 'Squizzy'. He was a lovely, cheerful man in early middle age who seemed to be looking forward to it as much as we were. He looked as if he had come straight out of a comic turn as a fall guy. He was always smiling, he had a round face and, although he was short, he more than made up for his lack of inches by an ample girth. He rapidly became our staunchest ally and was delighted to have the job of looking after David Gower and Phil Edmonds. We knew we were in for special treatment.

When the formalities had been completed 'Squizzy' shot inside and began to open Great Western champagne bottles at a rare speed. Half on the platform and half inside the carriage we had an unofficial cocktail party with 'Squizzy' making sure that none of us ever had an empty glass. I have no idea what the other passengers made of it all and some of them were peering at us out of the windows looking, I thought, a trifle anxious. It was a quarter to seven before anyone suggested that the train had an appointment in Kalgoorlie the following evening and so those who were staying in Adelaide climbed down onto the platform, the whistle blew and slowly we rattled our way out of the station.

It was the beginning of a journey I would not have missed for the world. The full distance from Sydney to Perth by way of Broken Hill, Adelaide, Port Augusta and Kalgoorlie is 3,959 kilometres and the journey takes sixty-seven hours. The train leaves Sydney on the Sunday afternoon and arrives in Perth in time for an early breakfast on the Wednesday. From the moment the doors were slammed in Adelaide and the wheels began to turn we were enveloped by an all-pervading sense of timelessness. The cabins were small and functional while the loo, shower and basin were a miracle of modern design. It was extraordinary that all three could fit into such a small space. The only problem was that it needed a first-class honours degree in engineering before you were able to use them, for somehow they all seemed to fold up into each other and to unravel them was almost impossible. In the end I found it easier to walk to the loo at the end of the carriage.

I found on my comfortable but narrow bed a copy of *Gone on the Ghan* by Derek Whitelock, a book about the great railway journeys of Australia. The Ghan is the name of the train which makes the journey from Adelaide to Alice Springs. A hundred years ago camels were the main beasts of burden in the desert and the camel drivers, most of whom came from Pakistan, would travel by train to the railhead at Marree, an outback town on the way to Alice Springs. The navvies, whose geography was less than exact, called the train the Afghan Express. This soon became the Ghan. I also found on my bed what I imagine is the Australian Railways tie. It is dark blue with small pink camels all over it which, I suppose, makes a change from pink elephants.

Our train was called the Indian Pacific for the excellent reason that it runs from the Pacific Ocean on the east coast to the Indian Ocean on the west coast – and back again. Express was something of a misnomer for it seldom moved along at more than 100 kilometres an hour and often at considerably less, especially over the Nullarbor itself where the intense heat can play tricks with the rails. After showing us to our cabins, 'Squizzy' marched us along to the bar which was presided over by Trevor who was not only extremely friendly but also a highly competent operator. If we had any complaints as far as his department was concerned, it was not that there was any shortage of supplies, it was just that the quality of the vino might have been better. The entire stock of dry white wine consisted of six half bottles of Houghton's White Burgundy and we had dealt with that some considerable time before going to our respective pews in the dining car. By then we had moved on to a Rhine Riesling of more dubious parentage. I kicked myself for not bringing our own supplies. Maybe the normal clientele were less demanding or maybe they preferred the hard stuff or simply did not have such outrageous thirsts. Anyway, with half a bottle of white Burgundy each we sat on the sofas in the bar and reviewed our lot.

Peter West drew thoughtfully on his first pipe of the journey while reflecting on how different life was that evening from the life he would have been leading at home tucked away in the Cotswolds. Peter was looking forward to the journey as much as I was and his enthusiasm for everything was one of the joys of the whole tour. Phil Edmonds had walked into the bar in that purposeful way of his with a copy of Robert Lacey's *Ford* under his arm; he had that world-weary, seen-it-all-before look on his face which those who watch him play cricket know so well. David Gower seemed rather drained and must have been thankful to be away, at least momentarily, from the treadmill cricket tours can so easily become. He had not started the tour well and was the odd man out, the captain who had just been sacked. Scyld Berry sipped away, looking part inscrutable, part scholarly with a mildly sardonic smile on his lips. His glasses give him that look of the absent-minded professor. Adrian Murrell was busily exploring the endless photographic possibilities which lay ahead before helping me to load a film into my new camera which was to come to such a sad end later in the tour at Watson's Bay in Sydney. Various members of the England side threw me into the water and my camera was in my pocket.

The first sitting for dinner, began depressingly early, was already under way but it had been arranged on the platform in Adelaide that we would be part of the second sitting for every meal. This meant an eight o'clock dinner. While sitting in the bar we got our first glimpse of some of our fellow first-class passengers. Some had come all the way from Sydney and were travelling as we were, just for the hell of it. There were some

Americans who were 'doing' Australia and there were a few on board who would do anything rather than fly. Everyone seemed in pretty good form and all were determined to have a good time. To start with our fellow passengers did not quite understand why such a fuss was being made of us although, as the journey went on, autograph books began to appear.

At first, we moved slowly through the neat, green suburbs of Adelaide, going almost due north for five hours along the coast to Port Augusta. The light held for more than an hour while the suburbs were overtaken by vast prairies of wheat. Our last look as dusk turned into night was of the fertile coastal strip. 'Squizzy' now appeared to tell us that it was time for dinner and led us to the two tables at the far end of the dining car which were to be ours for the journey. We were next door to the kitchen and 'Squizzy' brought us our food amid a constant stream of stories about life on the Indian Pacific. We had vegetable soup which probably came out of a packet, curried prawns and an excellent steak washed down by the aforementioned Rhine Riesling and plenty of half bottles of robust red wine which slipped down easily even if it tasted a trifle rusty. Although the train proceeded at a leisurely rate, it wobbled about a fair bit and, at intervals, wine and then coffee slurped over the edge of glasses and cups. The only person who was wholly unaffected by any sudden movement was 'Squizzy' who would have won a gold medal for carrying four full bowls of soup at the same time without ever spilling as much as a drop and never drawing breath as he moved at full speed. It was a masterful performance.

During dinner I had the temerity to tell Edmonds that I thought he had bowled badly against South Australia. He was horrified and told me that he considered he had bowled rather well and that I had merely noticed his figures of nought for plenty in the South Australian second innings and had assumed he had bowled badly. At one point he turned to Gower and quietly observed how appalling it was that such uninformed criticism would travel round the world. Peter West inclined to Edmonds's side and so, after a while, I felt it was tactful to change the conversation – but I still don't think he bowled very well.

As we have seen, Phil Edmonds is always great value and highly entertaining. He is a fearless talker which is refreshing for he is never afraid to voice his opinions, in sharp contrast to most cricketers when talking to the media. He has views on almost everything and enjoys an outlet for them. He is seldom plagued with self-doubt and made no secret of the fact that he considered that he should be captain of England.

While Edmonds expounded upon all manner of things at the dinner table, David Gower sat beside him deep in thought. When we made this journey Gower was in a muddle with his thinking and understandably so. More than anything, he seemed to be having a crisis of identity and it was so important that, as the sacked captain, he should once again be made to feel he belonged if the best was to be got out of him. It was stupid of those concerned not to include him on the tour committee. A more outgoing chap might not have felt it in the same way. Eventually, he was co-opted onto the committee but his troubles were to grow worse before they improved.

After dinner we returned to the bar and found that word had already got around for Gower and Edmonds had to cope with plenty of requests for autographs. By then, most of us were in excellent form and much was said with a fair degree of intensity as characters we all knew were discussed and not, I hope, assassinated. We received a welcome interruption when the train drew into Port Augusta and, at 'Squizzy's' suggestion, we all stretched our legs on the platform. Then came a long burst on the whistle, the doors slammed and we were off again into the night. I think we had a final drink and then it was time for bed. My cabin produced a narrow but comfortable mattress although I now found it was beyond me to try and unravel the puzzles set by my loo, basin and shower. I eventually got to grips with all of this in the morning only to find that it was to no avail for in their hurry to put on the extra coach in Adelaide they had forgotten to fill up the water tank, so it was in every sense a dry carriage.

It was just after six o'clock in the morning when I woke; the quiet rumble of the train reminded me of where I was and the pain in my head of what I had done. Rather reluctantly, I crawled to the end of my bed and turned the handle to open the blinds. The scene outside took my breath away. Scorched red earth and rough scrub stretched away to the horizon and beyond. This was the Nullarbor Plain in all its infernal glory and I lay there mesmerized. I have never seen anything so bleak, so dry, so arid and so desolate. It was desert piled on desert, a vast nothingness which reached away to the very curvature of the earth itself. It was then, for the first time maybe, that I realized the size of Australia. It was an eerie spectacle and, as I looked out from my air-conditioned hutch, I could sense an intense heat engulfing me. I was sure as I knelt there that I could feel the red dust creeping up my nostrils. I stood up and opened the door into the corridor and, sure enough, there it was on the other side too, flashing past as if it was on some giant cinema screen. But it was not flashing past, it was all the same for mile after mile, hour after hour. The only sign of civilization, apart from the railway train itself, was the row of telegraph poles beside the line. Otherwise it was an awe-inspiring nothing that did not change but was, nevertheless, incredible.

'Squizzy' herded us in to breakfast and produced a veritable feast of fruit juices and eggs and bacon, sausages and mushrooms. Conversationally, he was at the top of his form and left all of us far behind. Breakfast tasted delicious and Edmonds ploughed his way on through *Ford*; Peter West had brought a notebook with him and, pipe at the ready, was already dreaming up the golden phrases for the following day's *Daily*

Telegraph in London. They were going well, too, for I can remember the smile on his lips. From where we were sitting it seemed extraordinary that the earth's communications system had been developed to the stage where anything written while we were having breakfast in the middle of the Nullarbor had better than a one in a million chance of being transmitted to London before nightfall. The telephone in Kalgoorlie was all that was needed.

While serving the eggs, bacon, coffee and toast, 'Squizzy' prepared us for our landfall at Cook in mid-morning. Cook is a tiny habitation in the middle of the desert just before crossing from South Australia to Western Australia. It lies at the start of what is known locally as the 'Long Straight', the longest stretch of dead-straight railway line in the world. It runs for 478 kilometres. Although connected to the outside world by a healthy railway line, Cook brings a new meaning to the phrase, 'the back of beyond'. There are fewer than 100 people living in the village and they are employed either by the Australian Railways or by Telecom. 'Squizzy' himself had lived in Cook for a year as a boy when his father had been stationed there by the Railways. You could tell from the way he spoke that Cook was rather special to him, although I daresay he was grateful not to be still living there. His present home was Port Pirie between Adelaide and Port Augusta. The Railways were 'Squizzy's' life and I am sure he would never want to change it. Being the character he is, he does a wonderful PR job for the Indian Pacific for he is one of those lovely men with the ability to make everyone his friend. Without him, we would not have enjoyed the journey half so much.

'Squizzy' told us that Cook had recently become the proud possessor of a modern swimming pool. This had been paid for by the small souvenir stall at the station, in that every dollar which was passed over the counter at the stall had been matched by a present of four more from the South Australian government. He admitted that Cook was dusty and hot but, from the way he spoke, there was obviously a strong sense of pride amongst those who live in this small outpost. As he spoke, I continued to gaze, mesmerized, through the window. It was still the same – bright red, dusty and hot wherever you looked – and, by now, I had realized how aptly the Nullarbor had been named for not only was there not a tree in sight, there was nothing over eighteen inches.

In mid-egg Gower said it all. He looked up and smiled, slightly nervously, at no one in particular and said simply, 'It's so relaxing. It's different from the noise and the rush of airports and aeroplanes.' I think I would not have been the only one who would have been happy if the journey had gone on for another couple of days.

After breakfast we made our way back to our cabins and, while I was tidying up, an announcement came over the public-address system. A voice told us that, as this was the day of the Melbourne Cup which consumes

Australia in a way which makes the Derby at Epsom look like the answer to question one, it had been suggested by some of the passengers that the staff might like to run a sweepstake. We were then told, rather piously I thought, that they would do no such thing as it was against their principles but that, if any of the passengers wanted to organize one amongst themselves, it would have the approval of the management. When we returned to the bar everyone was making arrangements to organize a sweepstake and Trevor behind the bar was the focal point. He told me that the staff themselves were not allowed to buy tickets for, if they drew all the best horses, it would look as if the whole thing was a put-up job.

But our minds were now taken off the Melbourne Cup by the arrival of Cook. First, the train started to slow down and then, on the left-hand side, there was a dust track which had obviously been used by four-wheeled vehicles. A moment later I saw a dark-green station wagon known in Australia as a 'Ute', short for utility, parked on the track. Shortly after this came a decent-sized bungalow with a hint of a green bush by the front door and another parked car. This was set about 100 yards back from the railway line and was followed almost at once by a smaller, lower building with a corrugated-iron roof. Like everything else it was dusty and not entirely welcoming. Outside the front door stood a blackboard on an easel just as if it had come straight from the schoolroom and on it were printed in block capitals the two chilling words, 'Police Station'. Then there were more houses and a flash or two of green which belonged to more heavily watered bushes. As the train came to a halt I could see what was almost a village street behind the little station. There were people milling round and the souvenir stall was well manned.

We jumped down to the ground for there was no platform as such and, while most people flocked to the stall, Peter West and I set off across the dusty limestone to have a good look at Cook. It was marvellous to be able to stretch our legs and, after Peter had persuaded a veritable bonfire of smoke to gush from his pipe, we walked towards the back of the train and then turned right into a sort of street. As we turned away from the station we immediately passed two small, upright huts which looked as if they might be Mark One telephone kiosks or even portable loo cabins. They were attracting plenty of attention so we left them until last and set off intrepidly for the centre of Cook. It was only about fifty yards away and was identified by a piece of rock looking rather like a Henry Moore sculpture which had gone slightly adrift. On it a plaque celebrated the planting of sixty trees in Cook two years before. You could be forgiven for not thinking you were standing in the middle of a forest but a close inspection revealed that, indeed, small trees were growing outside several of the houses. With heavy watering they were, if not exactly flourishing, at least alive.

Peter and I walked on past the rock and, on our right just before the houses gave way to the desert, was the modern swimming pool which, although marvellously incongruous in such a setting, was, judging by the screams and yells, keeping the contemporary generation of young 'Squizzy's happily occupied. We then wandered back and turned our attention to the two 'telephone kiosks'. They must have been about ten feet tall and, standing side by side, had sturdy wooden doors with a small square hole cut at eye level with a long, narrow, barred window just above the lintel. They turned out to be Cook's two jailhouses and were of a considerable age. They are now nothing more than tourist attractions but, in the past, wrongdoers (usually drunks making a nuisance of themselves on the train) were locked up until another train came along to take them back to where they had come from. They helped create a strong flavour of the Wild West which enveloped Cook. But I think it might have taken quite a posse of sheriffs to have held Ned Kelly in such a contraption for any length of time.

Time was beginning to run out and so we paid a quick visit to the souvenir stall and, with great originality, we both bought a T-shirt which boasted a map of Australia on the front with Cook printed in the middle. While we were admiring our purchases and having a good look at our fellow passengers, most of whom we had not seen before for they were travelling in steerage, the local station master, dressed more like an upmarket cowboy than anything else, stepped forward to the side of the train, clasping the kind of large brass bell which used to summon us to meals at school. After a slight pause he rang it vigorously and we took our last photographs before jumping aboard. As we climbed in Phil Edmonds told me that I could think what I liked about his bowling in Adelaide – and laughed.

Cook had provided us with another interesting experience and now, as we returned to the desert, we were free to concentrate upon the Melbourne Cup. After that announcement over the intercom I was not at all sure that we were not letting the side down when, back in the bar, conversation again turned to sweepstakes. But Trevor announced again that he had every intention of organizing a sweep.

In fact, he ran two because the first was over-subscribed. I invested $10 and then settled down to read P.G. Wodehouse's *Carry on Jeeves* which I had bought in a second-hand bookshop in Adelaide. I cannot think of any occasion when Wodehouse does not make the most admirable of travelling companions; I had a total of eight of his books in my bag. I had to break off to listen to the commentary from Flemington and the excitement built up as At Talaq held off Rising Fear in the last furlong. Sheikh Hamdan al Maktoum had come to Australia to see his horse race. I had drawn Rising Fear and came out all square. As I collected my winnings from Trevor I wondered if there was any corner of the country which had not been invaded that day by the Melbourne Cup. I also wondered if there was any corner of the racing world which had not been conquered by the Maktoum family from Dubai.

Lunch in the form of a salad came next and, by now, our source of wine had almost run out. 'Squizzy' hoped we might be able to replenish our stocks at the point where the single track becomes two in order to allow trains to pass each other. There is a short stop and the staff exchange greetings but, unhappily on this particular occasion, they were unable to grab any more wine. There were only eight more hours to go. Lunch was followed by a kip and, at different times, Robert Lacey, Robert Ludlum (who had turned up in Adrian Murrell's hands) and P.G. Wodehouse were eagerly devoured. Westy sucked thoughtfully and intellectually at his pipe as he polished his literary gems while Scyld Berry contemplated a feature he was planning to write about David Gower. The scenery outside soon began to change although the track remained ramrod straight. There was now scrubby grass growing under the bushes and, every now and then, we saw signs of dusty humanity in the form of an occasional truck or cart track. The stark hopelessness of the desert began to disappear, too, slowly at first, but the country became friendlier and more recognizable. Then suddenly the scrub gave way in part to desiccated gum trees and we saw the occasional bird. My only regret was that I never saw a single kangaroo.

Then, it was the outskirts of Kalgoorlie and the shafts of the gold mines etched against the evening sky and, finally, the station and a taxi ride to a twentieth-century motel. I think we all had to shake ourselves back to the reality of a world which had to do with half volleys and off drives and left-arm spin however well or badly delivered. 'Squizzy' was given the tickets he wanted for the game the following day and we said a sad farewell for he had made a splendid companion for just over twenty-eight hours. I very much hope that if ever I make the journey again I shall find 'Squizzy' still in office. This was my first footfall in Kalgoorie since October 1968 when, in the company of cartoonist Paul Rigby, former England fast bowler, Peter Loader, and then cricket correspondent of the *Adelaide Advertiser*, Keith Butler, we stepped out one night through the backdoor of Hannan's Hotel into Hay Street and paid a strictly non-professional visit to one of the drums where Rigby was known and, for more than three hours, regaled the girls and their madame with stories from the outside world. Rigby had introduced me as Lord Henry FitzCounterpipe – but I have told that story at length elsewhere. This time I brought to Kalgoorlie more immediate memories of my first journey through a desert and, yes, as I write these words, I can still feel that dust on my tonsils.

— 7 —
Victory at Last

The Ashes series 1986–87 • England's cricket managers • the
Jackman affair in Guyana recalled • Lester Bird's start as a Test
commentator • Gatting and Stewart work well in tandem • a
crucial slip catch missed off Gower • Australia
outplayed • consumer demand for instant cricket • an
unlikely World Series Cup win for England • loner Bobby
Simpson as manager • a note on Australian cricket
writing • Allan Border, Australia's mainstay.

The Indian Pacific Express did not produce any magical powers of healing
and not only were England saved from a big defeat by Western Australia
by the weather which washed out the last day, but David Gower also
made nought in each innings. The side returned to Brisbane two days
before the start of the First Test Match with no form behind them and
their morale shattered. The brave words of Gatting and the cricket
manager, Micky Stewart, seemed to have an increasingly hollow ring to
them. On the other hand, the Australians were beginning to think that
they had as good as won the series. False impressions were being created
all round.

During the English summer of 1986 when New Zealand and India were
beating England there was a growing feeling that England needed a
permanent cricket manager. There had never before been such a job
although, during the second half of the seventies, Ken Barrington had
unofficially held the post. The Colonel, as he was known, had done a
marvellous job helping the young players in the England side and keeping
the respect of the older ones. Barrington was alternately coach, advisor,
confidant, nanny and, at times, disciplinarian too. He was, in so many
ways, an old-fashioned cricketer. No one had worked harder at his game
when he played and no one was shrewder when it came to helping players
try to sort out their problems. He was kind but firm and had much good
sense to impart. He had no greater supporter, for example, than Ian
Botham. Ken had once again become an integral part of English cricket
and its progress in the eighties seemed likely to depend to some extent on
him. The only mildly sour note that was struck was in Australia in 1979–
80 when Mike Brearley, who was captain, told Ken that he did not want

Bob Willis: even he could be the autocrat at times

(*Left*) Kim Hughes: his expression says it all after defeat at the Oval

(*Right*) Clive Lloyd: Paddington Bear to the end

Mr and Mrs Edmonds: nuptial bliss in front of the Taj Mahal

(*Left*) An impish Gavaskar acknowledging applause for a job well done during the MCC Bicentenary match

(*Right*) Mike Brearley: always purposeful and determined even when dismissed

Viv Richards: yes, man, a ten-star performer

Abdul Qadir and Imran Khan: and now, for our next trick

Imran Khan: handsome is as handsome does

Richard Hadlee: any idiot could see that was out

Viv Richards and Clive Lloyd: what's that idiot doing now?

(*Left*) Viv Richards' father: for those in peril on the sea

(*Right*) Allan Border: it looks bad enough out of just one eye

Phil Edmonds: another tycoon has sold at the top

David Gower: captaincy is not all it's written up to be

The Houston Astrodome: with football in progress

him changing players' techniques in the nets; to some extent, this compromised him. But Barrington was back as his own man when Botham took the side to the West Indies in 1980–81.

It was a depressing tour with a heavy defeat in the First Test and there was no one who took it more to heart than the cricket manager. The Guyana leg of the tour was disrupted when the Guyanese government declared Robin Jackman (who had replaced Bob Willis) *persona non grata* because of his frequent visits to South Africa and, as far as one could gather, because he had had the temerity to marry a South African wife. It was posturing by Forbes Burnham's Marxist government which was, at the time, making a point of trying to keep in favour with the Organization for African Unity.

The Second Test Match in Georgetown was cancelled, we all flew to Barbados and, after secret meetings between the Foreign Ministers of Barbados, Antigua and Jamaica (the countries hosting the remaining three Test Matches), the tour was allowed to continue. The Antiguan Foreign Minister, Lester Bird, whom I have mentioned earlier in relation to Graham Gooch during the 1985–86 tour of the West Indies, was also a cricket commentator in Antigua which was about to hold its first ever Test Match on the Recreation Ground in St John's. Lester Bird was himself about to become a Test Match commentator and, if that Test had been cancelled, perhaps he would never have become one. I would love to think that such considerations played a part in his thinking during those meetings in Barbados.

The Third Test went ahead at Kensington Oval, Barbados, Graham Gooch made a brilliant 100 on the first day, but the rest of the batting fell apart. That evening Ken Barrington, as disappointed as anyone, and his wife Anne went out to dinner with some friends. When they returned to the Hilton Hotel he sat down on his bed and, when his wife came out of the bathroom, she found that he had died of a massive heart attack. Cricket and an enormous number of people had lost a real friend.

The position of cricket manager was then filled for a time by Norman Gifford who never had quite the necessary stature. After Gifford, the job passed to Bob Willis who went to the West Indies with Gower's side in 1985–86. He had limited success as we have already seen. When, in 1986, it looked as though a permanent cricket manager would be appointed the front runners were Ray Illingworth and Warwickshire's David Brown. They were sounded out as to their availability and it appears that they both wanted the job only if given certain promises, one of which was that the manager and the captain would be the only selectors. This was unacceptable to the TCCB and Illingworth and Brown were not therefore selected. The Board eventually turned to Micky Stewart who had, for a number of years, been no more than a partially successful manager of Surrey. During the seventies several counties had appointed cricket managers but none had had great success. It was debatable whether they had a job to do. A strong captain would not want a manager to interfere and, if a county had a weak captain, their most urgent need was for a strong one.

Stewart, who had captained Surrey with great success, had played in eight Test Matches as an opening batsman and, while he was an excellent county cricketer, was probably not quite good enough at Test level. His lack of Test experience was eagerly seized upon by his critics and he was compared with Bobby Simpson who was Australia's full-time cricket manager and had played in sixty-two Test Matches. Stewart was given the job for one tour only and, if he was successful, was going to be offered a three-year contract on his return home.

Although the dismal results early in the tour hardly suggested it, Stewart and Gatting struck up an excellent partnership in Australia. Gatting was probably relieved to have some of the burdens of captaincy taken away from him while Stewart, in turn, was able to shape much of Gatting's thinking – indeed, to teach him a great many things about the game. Gatting has never suggested that on his own he is an especially imaginative thinker about the game. Stewart helped him here and also arranged the practices and, generally, took control of the cricket off the field. Gatting was happy that certain prerogatives of the captain had been taken over by the cricket manager. It may be that Gatting's long-term successor will not be so happy that his powers should be usurped in this way.

In Australia, the combination of Gatting and Stewart could not have been better and their most impressive performance came in Brisbane. They managed, in forty-eight hours, to lift the England party from a state of gloom to a condition of optimism and self-belief. One of Stewart's strengths on that tour was that, like Barrington, he kept it simple and was always cheerful. He talked logic and, in Australia, although a crucial member of the party he never allowed himself to become one of the boys. He kept a mental half pace away, much the best way if you are the team manager. It enabled him to be more dispassionate and not, therefore, to pull his punches at crucial moments. I am sure that even then many people looked forward to the chance of scoffing at Stewart if things went wrong. His inexperience at Test level and the fact that he had never played in Australia would not have been lost either on his opposite number, Bobby Simpson, who was also new to his job.

Australia's confidence was well illustrated when Allan Border won the toss for the eighth consecutive time and sent England in to bat on a pretty good pitch at Brisbane. England made 456 and went on to win by seven wickets when they bowled out Australia for 248 and 282. Not only did the England batsmen withstand Australia's two left-arm fast bowlers, Bruce Reid and Chris Matthews, they went on to out-play Australia in every aspect of the game. It was a remarkable turnaround of recent form. The principal England batting hero was Ian Botham who had been determined to make his mark on this tour. He was spurred on by England's poor showing in the early matches and took Gatting and Stewart's advice and encouragement to heart. I have no idea what was said at the traditional team dinner the night before that First Test Match. Doubtless the opposition was dissected, but the main job facing Gatting and Stewart was to try to reorganize the players' thinking. Whatever was said or done, that meeting changed the course of the tour. I have no doubt, too, that the ignominy of the situation acted as a motivation on all the players.

The only batsman to fail in Brisbane was Chris Broad and, for him, it was the only time in the series. He was the one batsman who was undone by the left arm over angle of delivery which had caused such trouble in the early matches; he was caught behind off Reid. Gatting, Athey and Lamb all made important contributions but, when Athey and Lamb were out before a run had been scored on the second morning, Australia were back in the match.

One of the most significant events of the series occurred between the fall of these two wickets. Athey was LBW to the first ball of the day and David Gower took his place fresh from his two noughts in Perth. In the third over of the morning he faced Merv Hughes who bowled short and outside the off stump. Gower fenced airily and the ball flew off the edge in the air to the right of third slip. Chris Matthews, playing his first Test Match, is a big man and a rather cumbersome mover. At the last moment he snatched at the ball with both hands and dropped it.

If that catch had stuck, the course of this Test Match would have changed, and, for Gower, it would have been his third successive nought; goodness knows what that would have done for his confidence. Like all good batsmen when they are out of form, the first thing to go is the footwork and for some time he carved away outside the off stump without moving his feet. He threw his bat into drives when the ball was pitched up, upper-cut the ball over gulley and the slips and edged it as well. Gradually, he began to find the middle with rather more regularity, however, and as his confidence returned so did his footwork. He pulled Steve Waugh, he whipped Hughes through mid-wicket and he pulled Reid, reaching a brave but not especially glorious 50, before pulling Chris Matthews hard to mid-wicket. It was, nonetheless, a significant innings as we shall see.

While Gower was stuttering into a start, Botham came in when Lamb was out and his determination was so great, as was his refusal to take a risk, that one sensed that we were in for something special. He took full advantage of anything loose as he drove and played the ball powerfully away off his legs. He once slashed Hughes over square third man for 6 but somehow, in his mood, it was not a risk. He hooked powerfully and for once was not content to deal predominantly in boundaries. When a straight drive for 2 off Hughes brought him to his 100 he had been batting for 217 minutes, a long time for Botham, and had hit only ten fours and a 6 – statistics which tell a story. His 138 was the most disciplined innings he had ever played for England and it made almost sure of England's victory in that First Test Match.

It was now Australia's turn to be demoralized for, having sent England in, they had watched them spend almost two full days amassing 456. That evening, Boon pulled DeFreitas to mid-wicket and the next day Graham Dilley, with five for 68, was the main reason that Australia subsided to 248 all out and followed on 208 runs behind. Geoff Marsh, who had made a typically determined 50 in the first innings, made a most worthy 100 in the second when long periods of defence were enlightened by the occasional lovely off-drive. No one could stay with him, however, and this time it was Emburey who collected five wickets. England needed 75 to win and lost three wickets in getting there. It had been an overwhelming victory which stunned the Australians who must have left Brisbane feeling rather as England did when they arrived the week before from Perth.

After that, the story of the rest of the series is quickly told for the psychological advantage never shifted, at least until the Ashes had been retained by England, and then only briefly. Strange though it may seem, after the heady triumph in Brisbane, England flew down to Newcastle and were beaten in just over three days by eight wickets by New South Wales. It was a poor pitch made for seam bowlers and England amassed 181 and 82; events suggested that some of the players were still thinking about Brisbane. The New South Wales bowlers knew the pitch and also had some players with a point to prove to the Australian selectors.

The Second Test in Perth saw England amass 592 for eight after winning the toss, with Broad, Gower at his brilliant best, and Richards (who was lucky to hold his place as wicket-keeper) scoring hundreds, and Athey missing his by 4 runs. Thanks to another wonderful 100 by Border, who was last out for 125, Australia saved the follow-on and after that had little difficulty in saving the match.

Australia won the toss in the Third Test in Adelaide and, with Boon making a spirited 100 and the most of the others contributing, went past 500. Broad then made his customary 100 and Gatting added another, taking them to 450. The third match was also drawn. The Boxing Day Test in Melbourne was a comprehensive disaster for Australia who were put in on the first day and bowled out for 141. Another 100 by Broad took England to 349 and, with scarcely a fight, Australia lost before the end of the third day by an innings and 14 runs.

The Test series was then interrupted by a one-day competition in Perth to celebrate the America's Cup races. England beat Pakistan in the final after the West Indies had been beaten by both finalists in the qualifying round – another sign of their increasing vulnerability.

The Fifth Test was now played in Sydney on a pitch which increasingly took spin. Dean Jones effectively won the match with a brilliant innings for Australia after Border had won an important toss. Jones finished with 184 not out, taking Australia to 343. The spinners claimed twenty-two of the last thirty wickets to fall and, in spite of a fighting innings of 96 by Gatting, a target of 320 was too much for England and Australia won by 55 runs.

The Australian season ended, as it always does, with the Benson and Hedges World Series Cup; England, Australia and the West Indies cavorted around the country playing fourteen one-day games in twenty-five days. Since the peace treaty between World Series cricket and the Australian Cricket Board, there are those in powerful positions in Australian cricket who seem to regard this one-day competition as the virility symbol of the Australian game.

Of course, one-day cricket is important and has its place but, since the end of December, we had had to sit through twenty-one one-day internationals, including the Perth competition. By the end, it had become a bore and no one finds this more than the players who, each year, are profoundly thankful if the same side wins the first two of the best-of-three finals making the third unnecessary.

The one-day competition, which was designed originally for a television audience, also attracts considerable crowds; it therefore makes a big profit for the ACB (always the main purpose of this type of cricket) which was why it was invented in the first place in England in the early 1960s. It has, too, fulfilled a social need in that people today have not the time or the money to watch a five-day Test Match nor, many of them, the inclination to watch something which may have an inconclusive result at the end of it all. It is easy to understand the attraction of limited-over cricket which produces a result in one day and all the fun of the fair along the way. It has introduced a new audience to the game which must be a good thing, even if one-day crowds fall more into the pattern of football crowds in England. We live in a violent society and one-day cricket is a product of that society. This is an age which requires instant everything and instant cricket is one by-product.

Keith Miller and Ray Lindwall did not behave in the forties as Dennis Lillee and Jeff Thomson did thirty years later, for society would not have tolerated it. The same comparison could be made on the tennis circuit with Rosewall and Hoad in the fifties and McEnroe and Connors at the present time. One-day cricket would probably not have made the same impact then as it does now.

There is, undoubtedly, a place for the one-day game but it seems wrong that, while the crowds enjoy the World Series Cup in Australia, the players find it a bore and cannot wait for the end. If anyone doubts this, just turn up on an aeroplane which is lifting the contestants one morning towards the end of the competition from, say, Melbourne to Sydney and hear what they have to say. The Australian players feel the same as those from overseas. It is then that you realize how a modern cricket season can become a treadmill. The argument will be put forward that they are well paid, as if this is a justification on its own. I would have thought that job satisfaction is also important if the players are to be seen at their best. This seems to me to be a classical situation of the tail wagging the dog. I am sure nothing will be done about it and I can understand the indignation the Australian authorities show when a highly profitable brain-child of theirs is criticized – especially by a foreigner.

The 1986–87 competition was won in the end by England who, halfway through, looked almost certain not to qualify. The crucial qualifying game was played in Devonport in Tasmania between England and the West Indies just before the finals. Whoever won it would go through to play Australia. The West Indies put England in to bat and only Broad and Lamb made any headway against the fast bowlers on a pitch with a variable bounce.

A target of 178 would surely not test the West Indies, but they were without Gordon Greenidge and Desmond Haynes who were both unfit and, as a result, they were soon two wickets down for very few. Larry Gomes then flicked Botham to square leg and Viv Richards aimed to cut Botham and succeeded in dragging the ball into his stumps – not helped by the low bounce. Botham's joy was unconfined for it is not often that he triumphs over his former Somerset colleague. Richards was the fourth out at 73 in the twenty-ninth over and, from that moment, the West Indies never looked like winning in spite of some brave blows by Malcolm Marshall. The innings finally fell in a heap when John Emburey took three wickets in the forty-eighth over, all of them with full tosses, and England had won by 29 runs.

The West Indies were captained by Lloyd when they lost the 1983 World Cup final to India by 43 runs when they were chasing 183. Lloyd was again in charge in Adelaide in 1981–82 when the West Indies were asked to score just 141 to beat Pakistan and were beaten by 8 runs. On those two occasions one felt it was nothing more than an accident of war; at Devonport I felt that all was not well with the side.

England, having got their second wind in Devonport, went to Melbourne and beat Australia by six wickets after Botham had blasted 71 runs off fifty-two balls at the start of the innings. The second final in Sydney was a better game. England made 187 for nine and then bowled splendidly to restrict Australia to 179 for eight and so won by 8 runs. That third final in Melbourne, to general relief, was not needed. It had been a clean sweep for England who had won the Ashes, the Perth competition and now the World Series Cup. For Australia, a summer which had appeared to begin so brilliantly with England's failures before the First Test had ended dismally and they had nothing whatever to show for their pains.

We have already looked at the two cricket managers, Stewart and Simpson, before the series began. Now, at the end of it, Stewart returned home in triumph to be welcomed by a three-year contract while Simpson was left to ponder what went wrong. Stewart had worked with a terrier-like enthusiasm with his players, lucky to have a captain who did not get in his way and a manager, Peter Lush, who never tried to interfere in cricketing matters. Stewart never made his advice seem too complicated and he won the respect of the players. He must take great credit for the way in which he helped Gatting create a good atmosphere before the First Test Match after the disastrous build-up matches. Stewart seemed a straightforward character with a slight twinkle even if he has become a past master at avoiding direct questions in front of a microphone. He was also immensely loyal to his players which is so important. No team victory like this can ever be the responsibility of any one man, for everyone has a part to play, but no one could have fulfilled his part better in Australia than Stewart.

Simpson, on the other hand, was a more enigmatic figure during that series. He is self-protective to the point of obsession – try criticizing him and see the result. I did just this for the Herald and Weekly Times Group, for which I was writing, after Australia's defeat in the Fourth Test in Melbourne. We all then gathered in Perth for the one-day competition and I was staying in the Perth Sheraton, as were the Australians and many of the distinguished cricket administrators who had flown in from all parts of the world for that week's cricket. I was talking, one day, to John Warr, the next president of MCC, in the lobby of the hotel, and he was telling me his latest unrepeatable funny story when Simpson walked past, interrupted us and had a big go at me for what I had written; his tones suggested my criticisms had hit home. I returned the compliment gratefully at the end of the celebratory dinner in the same hotel later in the week, when Simpson was talking to the chairman of the Australian selectors, Laurie Sawle, so I suppose honours were about even.

There is a great camaraderie among former Australian Test cricketers, of which Simpson seems to be left out. He was a wonderful opening batsman, a good leg spinner, and, maybe, the best first slip catcher ever. Like so many, he played the game in keeping with his character. If he played above all for himself, he was not unlike many of the outstanding players down the years. He was an effective captain, although he has not left behind feelings of deep loyalty with many of those who played under him for Australia and New South Wales. Perhaps he played it too much his own way.

Simpson first retired from Test cricket in 1967 at the age of thirty-one and then returned to captain the official Australian side in 1977–78 when the formation of World Series Cricket caused the split in Australian cricket. Rumour has it that Simpson had been approached by those setting up World Series Cricket to do the organizational job that was eventually done so ably by Richie Benaud. Rumour goes on to say that he turned it down because he felt it would not work. When World Series Cricket had been set up Simpson accepted the Australian Cricket Board's invitation to captain Australia against India and then to take the side to the West Indies.

As a player he made a remarkable return, making two 100s in the series against India and taking Australia to victory by three matches to two in a thrilling series. The tour of the West Indies which I have described in some detail in *The Packer Affair* was bedevilled by the battles between World Series Cricket and the West Indies Cricket Board of Control. The non-World Series Cricket Australia played and lost the first two Test Matches against the World Series Cricket West Indies side. The WSC West Indian players then pulled out of the series and Australia won against a weaker West Indian side in Georgetown, lost in Port of Spain and were prevented from winning the final match in Jamaica by a riot. Simpson had done an important job for the Australian Cricket Board, although the same doubts about him remained with some of his players. It looked as if he would captain Australia the following season against England but, in the event, he did not agree to do so. One heard that he wanted a guarantee from the Australian Cricket Board that he would captain the side for the whole series and that they were not prepared to give this. It was a sad end, therefore, to a gallant comeback.

Graham Yallop was chosen as his successor against Mike Brearley's first side in 1978–79. In choosing Yallop, the selectors passed over the claims of John Inverarity, a decision which was to cost them dear over the next few years. Inverarity was the Brearley of Australian cricket and, although he would have been an untypical Australian choice – he was then thirty-four – in the circumstances I believe that, had Inverarity been in charge when the Australian Cricket Board and World Series Cricket came together, the peace treaty and subsequent relations between the two sides would have been very much easier.

No coach or cricket manager could have better cricket credentials than Simpson but, in that series against England, he was unable to produce the results. It may have been harder for him than Stewart in that he had inherited Allan Border as captain. Border had been in charge for two years, had developed his own way of doing things, and may have been mildly suspicious of Simpson at the outset. Simpson had, however, been in charge on the short tour of New Zealand earlier in the year while Bob Merriman completed his last tour as permanent Australian team manager. By the time the England series began, the Australians would have been familiar with Simpson's methods.

The likelihood must be that Simpson, with the rest of the Australian side, was caught on the hop by England's disappointing build-up to Brisbane. They were taken unawares. For whatever reason, Border and

Simpson were unable to work the miracle on Australia which Gatting and Stewart had managed with England. Australia had grown very accustomed to losing over the previous year or two and it can be a difficult habit to break. England had lost their last three Test series before coming to Australia, but the players would have been all too aware of their overwhelming victory against Australia in England in 1985. Their habit of losing was not as deeply ingrained.

Hundreds by Border, as they normally do, prevented Australia from getting into bad trouble in the Second and Third Tests, but then in Melbourne they fell apart. A side that disintegrates as Australia did in that match has problems and, although he might want to blame it on the players or conditions (a natural reaction for anyone who is watching his back), the cricket manager could hardly claim that his job was going well. It was then that Simpson and I had our verbal confrontation in Perth. Australia went on to win the toss in Sydney, a ground where it is important to bat first, and the Fifth Test Match with it. But in all honesty, they were a trifle flattered by what was, in the end, only a 2–1 margin of defeat in the Ashes series. As we have seen, they went on to lose in the finals of the World Series Cup to England.

While it is not possible to know what goes on behind closed dressing-room doors, maybe it took Simpson longer than he anticipated to find the right approach to his side. He seemed to have a greater effect on the Australians later in the year in the World Cup in India although, by then, it was easier for him as one or two of his former charges – who may have found it difficult to play a team game – had not been selected.

It was another most disappointing season for Allan Border who, apart from Test Matches at the Sydney Cricket Ground and Lord's, had presided over almost unrelieved gloom in the Australian dressing-room. There had been times when he had had to be talked out of giving up the job. Border's own performance with the bat in this time has been extraordinary. Singlehandedly, he had saved Australia on countless occasions and it has been remarkable how he has fought on, although it must have been deeply discouraging for him to see how little support he sometimes received from his colleagues and indeed, at times, how little resolution some appeared to show. Border is a fiercely determined individual. He is not an extrovert and has probably had problems in communicating with his side. When things were going badly he was a lone figure.

It was interesting to see the change in him after Australia's World Cup victory and Australia's success after that against New Zealand and Sri Lanka in 1987–88. He was the obvious choice to take over when Hughes resigned, not because he had proved himself a good captain – he had only just succeeded Greg Chappell as captain of Queensland – but because he was the only realistic choice. He has not liked criticism in the press and I remember, during his first Test Match since taking over from Kim Hughes in 1984–85, going to his hotel room in Adelaide to interview him for the BBC. He had not liked something that I had written in the *Australian*, so he told me that he felt it was no help to his team. I tried to point out that my job was not to try to be a help to the Australian side but to be objective. He seemed to feel that, as I was writing in an Australian paper, I had a duty to the Australian side.

This raises an interesting question and highlights an essential difference in the cricket writing between some Australian papers and their English counterparts. The tabloids in both countries deal, understandably, in quotes whenever they can. In Australia the quality papers, the broadsheets, deal as much in quotes as the tabloids and, indeed, their writers rush off at the end of a day's play to interview some player or other or the captain if possible. An Australian captain is a most important source of copy because, apparently, the punters who buy the papers are dead set on reading what one or more of the participants think about that day's play. Because they are so closely involved with the game it is not easy for them to be objective. I would have thought that if an experienced writer, using his own name, was writing a piece, his readers would want first and foremost to know what he himself thought of that day's play.

In England, in the quality papers, the number one cricket correspondents write their own assessments. In these days of increasing news consciousness, the broadsheets in England have a man at the ground who writes a second piece and deals with the quotes and any other off-the-field points of interest. The danger of having to rely so consistently on the captain for his comments is that journalists are naturally loath to jeopardize their lines of supply and so, inadvertently, become the mouthpiece of the captain or, indeed, the manager. It is a situation which can lead to fewer and fewer cricket writers who are independent and able to say, at all times, what they truly think. Border's concern that what I had written was no help for his side probably stems from this situation.

Before we leave Border for the time being it is as a batsman, rather than a captain, that he will be longest remembered. Although he is not an especially graceful left-hander – pugnacious is more the word – he has some strokes which he plays as well as anyone. He drives beautifully through the covers off both fast and slow bowlers, he is an outstanding player of spin, he hooks well and has a powerful square cut. His defence is compact and well ordered and he must be in the top half-dozen batsmen in the world today; he does not, however, have the beauty or the glamour of Viv Richards, Gordon Greenidge, Martin Crowe, Sunil Gavaskar or Graeme Hick – I write this paragraph on the day that Hick scored 405 not out for Worcestershire against Somerset in 1988 and I think he must be included in this exalted company – although, being born in Zimbabwe, or Rhodesia as it then was, he will not be qualified to play for England until 1991, unless the rules are changed. Without Border in the period under discussion, Australia's record would not bear thinking about.

— 8 —

A Near Thing

Across the Tasman 1986–87: developing strength of New Zealand
under threat ● new fast bowlers a-plenty but where are West
Indies' young batsmen? ● enter Fred Goodall, centre
stage ● Viv Richards, critical intolerance at a critical
time ● umpire Goodall in West Indian confrontation.

If there's one thing I can't stand in Australia, which has become my
second home, it is their patronizing, dismissive attitude towards New
Zealand. I have been to New Zealand many times and have always hugely
enjoyed the country, the people, the generous hospitality and the great
friendship I have found there. It is, of course, different from Australia just
as any two countries have different characteristics. By their refusal to
acknowledge New Zealand cricket and to play Test Matches on either side
of the Tasman for so long, Australia held back its development. They sent
a side there to play one Test Match immediately after the Second World
War; this was won in two days. But it was not until 1973–74 that series
between the two countries became regular sporting events. Australia has
always had a lofty attitude towards its southernmost neighbour, border-
ing on contempt. I suppose as a foreigner it is none of my business but it
amuses me to say at a dinner party in Sydney, for example, 'You know,
these New Zealand white wines are leaving the Australian wines far
behind,' and to watch the result. It's like pulling the pin out of a hand-
grenade.

Since the recent restart of cricketing relations, New Zealand has not
done at all badly against Australia and, in general terms during the 1980s,
has more than held its own on the global stage. I have already written of
the enormous part played by Richard Hadlee and, in this chapter, there is
a chance to mention a few of the others. New Zealand has always
produced brilliant individuals and the skills and influence of Tom
Lowry, Stuart Dempster, Walter Hadlee, Martin Donnelly, John Reid,
Bert Sutcliffe, and others, have been rewarded, if belatedly, in the last
decade. More recently, they have produced such players as Bevan,
Congdon, Bruce Taylor, Hedley Howarth, Glenn Turner, Ken
Wadsworth, John Wright and Martin Crowe, in addition to Richard
Hadlee who would have been welcomed by any side in the world.

In the old days New Zealand had their sprinkling of brilliant performers, but the other members of the side did not play to a high enough level of consistency. A side is said to be as strong as its weakest link and, in recent years, that weakest link has considerably strengthened. There has been a greater discipline in New Zealand cricket, partly as a result of a number of their leading players taking part in English county cricket, the most demanding domestic competition of all. There have been those, too, who have had important experience in the leagues in the north of England. There is also a greater professionalism about New Zealand's domestic cricket these days which is reflected in their national performances.

While Australia's attitude to New Zealand's cricket has tended to be dismissive, it has ensured that beating Australia has been at the top of New Zealand's list of priorities. It was important to them to win that cantankerous series against the West Indies in 1980–81, but even that would not have been half so sweet as defeating Australia at Christchurch in March 1974. The ultimate triumph came in 1985–86 when New Zealand won its first ever series in Australia by two matches to one. Their First Test victory in England in 1983 at Headingley was another moment of rare triumph; I shall never forget the smiling face of Walter Hadlee, Richard's father, on the balcony of the pavilion afterwards, which seemed to say, 'I never thought I would live to see the day.' Their first victory in a series in England followed three years later in 1986.

By then the bits-and-pieces players were really pulling their weight. Scarcely a match went by without a telling contribution from John Bracewell, Ian Smith, Bruce Edgar, Jeremy Coney or Stephen Boock. It was off-spinner Bracewell's 100 at Trent Bridge in 1986 that made sure that New Zealand won that match. While New Zealand have had ten years of sometimes heady success it looks now as if they may be in for a leaner period while they rebuild. Jeremy Coney, such a successful captain, has retired to become a highly amusing and articulate expert commentator on Radio New Zealand; Bruce Edgar has finished with Test cricket; John Reid also decided that he had had enough and one or two of the others are getting older. Hadlee and Euan Chatfield are both in their upper thirties, Wright only slightly younger, although now that he has the captaincy my guess is that he will do it well and maintain his interest. It will also be good for New Zealand cricket if Martin Crowe does not have the captaincy thrust on him for a few more years yet.

The bowling will be the main worry, for Hadlee and Chatfield are beginning to live on borrowed time, Danny Morrison, for all his promise, is not learning very fast, Bracewell is no longer such a consistent off-spinner, left-arm spinner Boock has retired and replacements do not seem to be coming through. The batting is better for, during the 1987–88 season, two players, Andrew Jones and Mark Greatbatch, established themselves as Test batsmen, while two others, Chris Kuggeleijn and Robert Vance, showed promise. Ken Rutherford, batting down the order where he should always have been left, made 100 in the Third Test against England in March 1987 at Wellington, well enough to suggest that he will score several more. This was good news for Rutherford as, the year before, he had been destroyed by Joel Garner during the West Indies tour of New Zealand. He had also received a rough time in the Caribbean before that.

The short tour by the West Indies to New Zealand provided one or two pointers to the immediate future of West Indian cricket and also contained one very fortunate near miss. One of the fascinations of international cricket is the cyclical process which causes the fortunes of sides to rise and fall. Since 1976 the West Indies, with only the odd hiccup, have been on top. The other countries have climbed up and down the ladder without being able to make the final jump. As the period covered by this book unfolded we began to see a slight deterioration in the West Indies – they, of course, will resist the accusation saying that it is no more than a spurious rumour, and in England in 1988 it is as if they had a point. The fact is, though, that Lloyd has gone, which is significant, and that old age is creeping up on some of the other leading players. Viv Richards, Gordon Greenidge and Desmond Haynes no longer put it together as consistently as they once did. After so much success it is hardly surprising they may grow a trifle world-weary. The older you are, and the more successful, the harder it is to find the motivation to fight your way back to form.

In the Caribbean, too, a generation of small boys has wanted only to run in fast and bowl like Roberts and Holding, the architects of so much of the West Indies' recent success. Batting has not become a lost art but the days are long gone when all small boys picked up any piece of wood and said proudly, 'I'm Sobers' or 'I'm Kanhai,' although it is mystifying that the 'I'm Richards' brigade should not be stronger. Whatever the reason, with the notable exception of Carl Hooper the next generation of West Indian batsmen has not yet come through. Gus Logie, for all his brilliant fielding, has not developed into a major batsman, and Jeff Dujon has not quite fulfilled an unusual batting talent. In the World Cup in 1987 Phil Simmons looked a prospect but he suffered that terrible blow on the head against Gloucestershire in May 1988 and, at the moment, apart from Hooper, they do not seem to have batsmen who will stride into the West Indian side as of right in the way that Lloyd, Richards, Greenidge and Haynes have all done in the past. They could be short of runs for a while. While there are still plenty of fast bowlers around and Curtley Ambrose and Ian Bishop are the latest in the line, none as yet is of the calibre of Roberts and Holding and the West Indies had been taking longer to bowl sides out until Malcolm Marshall unleashed himself on the Englishmen in 1988 taking a record 35 wickets in the series.

After Lloyd walked off the Sydney Cricket Ground that day in January

1985 the West Indies, under Richards, won all five Test Matches against England in 1985–86 but, since then, they have seemed for a time rather more vulnerable and fragile without the familiar figure of Lloyd shuffling out at No 6 and standing lugubriously at first slip. Twelve months later this was seen to be so when, in the one-day competition in Perth to celebrate the America's Cup yacht races, the West Indies did not qualify for the finals. More surprisingly, perhaps, five weeks after that they did not reach the finals of the World Series Cup in Australia when their opponents were Australia and England. At the time, I asked a friend of mine who was close to the West Indies side, 'Who is Richards's right-hand man?' 'He doesn't have one,' came the reply. When I asked him who had been Lloyd's chief lieutenant I was told, 'There were never less than ten.'

The West Indies went to New Zealand after their fruitless visit to Australia, not without a certain degree of anxiety. It was their first tour of

New Zealand since that disastrous visit in 1979–80. When I had asked Clive Lloyd during his final Test Match in Sydney if he had any regrets about his career, this was the tour he was referring to when he said, 'I would like to have New Zealand over again.' Of course, memories grow dull in the space of seven years but the circumstances of that tour had been so unpleasant that they will never be completely forgotten. Richards himself had not been in New Zealand then, having gone home from Australia injured. A few of the players remained, including Michael Holding, normally such a gentle man, who with a sickening but graceful flourish had during the Dunedin Test Match spun round and kicked out the middle stump like some demented Nureyev after an appeal had gone against him. A further confrontation became a distinct possibility from the moment the New Zealand Cricket Council, with lamentable insensitivity, appointed Fred Goodall, the principal villain as far as the West Indies were concerned in 1979–80, to umpire the Second Test in Auckland.

Goodall, a schoolteacher by profession, has done yeoman service in the white coat for New Zealand down the years, but he is one of those problematical umpires who love to get in the game. He is forever running extravagantly off the ground with a tiresome display of athleticism or waving his arms at this and that. He is a great signaller of short runs, too, which shows either an eagle eye or, as W.S.Gilbert once wrote, 'affectation born of a morbid love of admiration'. In short, he has an officious and irritating bedside manner which is not helped by his pronounced strut. I have never known an umpire whose antics irritate so many spectators and one can only guess at what the players must feel. Every gesture he makes is exaggerated and it has reached the point where one cannot escape the impression that he sees his role more as a performer than as an arbiter of justice. Viv Richards has no small opinion of himself, either, and if ever two people were set on a collision course it was Richards and Goodall in the Second Test Match in Auckland.

It had been assumed for a long time that Richards would succeed Lloyd, rather as it was taken for granted that Gary Sobers would succeed Frank Worrell more than twenty years ago. In their different ways, Sobers and Richards both wore the mantle of the Crown Prince for a long time. One difference between the two was that if, say, Rohan Kanhai had taken over from Worrell, Sobers would have been happy to play under him and, indeed, did so when Kanhai took over briefly from Sobers himself in 1973 and 1974. If, on the other hand, Gordon Greenidge had followed Lloyd, Richards might well have decided to call it a day. Richards has been a brilliant batsman and, for some time, the greatest in the world; he has nearly 7,000 Test runs to his name, but Sobers was something more than that. He was quite simply the greatest all-rounder the game has ever known. He was a batsman who made 254 at Melbourne for the Rest of the World against Australia in 1971–72 in an innings which Don Bradman described as the greatest he had ever seen. Sobers scored 8,032 Test runs and took 235 wickets, bowling fast left arm over the wicket, orthodox and unorthodox left-arm spin; he also picked up a small matter of 109 catches besides. He was such a gentle character too who was always a great credit to the game. How well he deserved his knighthood.

Richards does not have the same easy-going, modest, unassuming character as Sobers. He has an altogether more flamboyant personality, a cricketer who is much more inclined to stroll onto the stage as a performer than to walk onto it as a participant. This is not to doubt Richards's involvement, which I know could not be more wholehearted, or his ability; it is simply to say that he has a greater sense of theatre and a larger ego than Sobers. In a sense, they are both the poor man made good; Richards is aware of it, Sobers does not appear to give it a thought. They have both enjoyed the physical rewards and the life styles cricket has brought them. Sober remains cheerfully, wittily and naturally unaffected by it all, while Richards lives a more ostentatious life of opulence. It is as if he enjoys, and is impressed by, the gold bangles which hang all over him as much as he hopes that others will be impressed. Of course, he is a quite brilliant batsman, it is just that he knows it and it is written large in every footstep he takes on a cricket field.

Richards has taken over the West Indian captaincy at a time when they are starting to rebuild the side. It remains to be seen whether he will be the ideal captain to be in charge of this delicate stage of his country's redevelopment. He has never been a man who has suffered gladly any weaknesses shown by his colleagues on the field of play. I well remember, during one of those interminable one-day matches which haunt the end of every Australian season, Richards captaining the West Indies in Melbourne. An opposing batsman skied the ball to square leg, both Marshall and Dujon went for the catch, got in each other's way and it was dropped. Richards was furious and made no secret of his feelings.

Worrell, Lloyd and, for that matter, Sobers, have shown that the one quality needed above all others by a captain of the West Indies – if he is to be successful – is calmness. It does not work for a captain who allows his feelings to run away with him. Richards gives the impression, too, that he knows all the answers and, in his first two years in the job, was not a captain obviously to seek opinions from the rest of his side, nor did his colleagues seem eager to come forward to offer their suggestions. This gives point to the remark quoted earlier that Richards does not have a right-hand man while Clive Lloyd always had ten. In May 1988 Richards led the West Indies to victory by two wickets in the Third and final Test Match against Pakistan in Bridgetown, enabling the West Indies to draw that series one all and avoid their first home defeat for fifteen years. By all accounts, he handled the side extremely well – he was ill and unable to play in the First Test which Pakistan won.

It was during this Third Test, though, that rumours were heard that the old inter-island and territorial rivalries were again being allowed to come to the fore. Richards is from Antigua and a few eyebrows were raised when Winston Benjamin, also from the Leeward Islands, was preferred to Patrick Patterson from Jamaica, a fierce proposition. Worrell, Lloyd and Sobers did not worry where players came from as long as the best side represented the West Indies which is, of course, a conglomerate of independent nations. If Richards is to have a long and happy reign as West Indian captain, he may have to suppress a few of his natural instincts.

Having said that, Richards showed in England in 1988 a much greater grasp of the requirements needed for the job. He saw England win all three of the one-day internationals and then succeeded in pulling his side together in admirable fashion for the Test series. He seemed a more forgiving figure in the field and one prepared to spend time helping his young players out of whom he brought the best, especially in fast bowler Curtley Ambrose. He may not perhaps be so popular in his own dressing room as his immediate predecessor, but it looked in England as if he had accepted advice and maybe criticism, and was on his way to becoming a worthy successor to Clive Lloyd. At the same time no praise can be too high for the way in which the former West Indian wicket-keeper, Jackie Hendricks, managed the side in England.

In New Zealand the First Test in Wellington saw some stirring cricket, first from the West Indian fast bowlers who seemed to have won the match and then from John Wright and Martin Crowe who, in their different styles, made marvellous 100s which enabled New Zealand to escape with a draw.

For those who like statistical oddities, in this second New Zealand innings Richards used one ball for 177 overs, by which time it was as soft and unruly as a rag doll – the reason given for this was that two of his bowlers were injured. It was a disappointing result for the West Indies who were let down in the end by some poor fielding; even a year earlier one felt that they would not have allowed New Zealand to escape. When they stepped out, therefore, at the start of the Second Test Match at Eden Park, Auckland, their own failure to win in Wellington would have left them in no mood to brook more nonsense. New Zealand, having escaped at the very end, would have been just as anxious not to get into the same position again.

As it happened, on the usual lifeless Auckland pitch it was rather a one-sided contest, with the West Indies winning by ten wickets, although another brilliant 100 by Martin Crowe kept them waiting until only 4.4 overs remained. Gordon Greenidge got his square cut working with devastating effect and made a double century; after that, the West Indian fast bowlers were irresistible. The moment many were certain would come occurred on the third day when Malcolm Marshall twice hit Jeff Crowe on the pads playing back.

A Near Thing

On the first occasion the appeal was unanimous and deafening. Umpire Goodall, leaning a long way forward, kept on looking down the pitch before eventually straightening up. The disbelief on the faces and in the actions of the West Indies, when they realized the appeal had been turned down, was remarkable and no one was more put out than Richards at first slip. For just a moment or two the world stood still and then, in an agony of discontent, Marshall walked back, disbelievingly, to his mark. Wicket-keeper and slips had an obviously disenchanted discussion and West Indian manager, Steve Camacho, looked worried and uncomfortable as he lit a cigarette in the stand. The over finished, Goodall strutted to square leg and Richards suppressed all that he felt and steadfastly made the journey from first slip to first slip without looking to either side. It had been a near miss, both for Jeff Crowe – the replay gave Goodall less than overwhelming support – and for international cricket as well.

The pressure notch was now a couple of turns tighter. A few minutes later Marshall ran in again to bowl to Jeff Crowe. Again he played back, again the ball smacked into the pad. The appeal could have been heard in Australia. All eyes flashed to umpire Goodall. Hands clasped behind his back, he again peered down the pitch before straightening decisively and flicking a coin from one hand to the other. As he was looking down the pitch you could see it begin to dawn on the West Indians that he was not going to give Crowe out.

When Goodall finally delivered the news, Richards was the very picture of discontent at first slip and glared around at everyone, hands upraised in disbelief, while the other fielders registered their silent but no less profound amazement. All eyes were now on Richards who, with that supremely confident, almost arrogant walk, strolled down the full length of the pitch to Goodall. Binoculars revealed that Richards began the conversation, but it is impossible to lipread from sideways on, which may have been just as well. For an appreciable, agonized moment the future of New Zealand/West Indies cricket remained suspended in thin air. Goodall, tempted though he may have been, probably felt that he had made his point and, after two more exchanges which it would be reasonable to guess were something less than lighthearted, Richards shrugged his shoulders and returned from whence he had come. The game continued, New Zealand were ruthlessly swept away and, at the end of the day, all those concerned wisely kept their own counsel. Phew! It was as close as that and Camacho must have been near to a place in the *Guinness Book of Records* for the fastest cigarette ever smoked.

Goodall and Richards are both intransigent men. From the moment Goodall was chosen to stand in that match it was a foregone conclusion that he would take the opportunity to make his point. It was no less certain that Richards would do all he could not to let him get away with it. Seven years earlier Clive Lloyd had simply stood at first slip and done nothing, allowing nature to take its course with awful results; these came to a point when Colin Croft charged into Goodall just as he was about to deliver a ball, a strange coincidence for a bowler who invariably moved to the outside edge of the crease in his delivery stride. In 1987, Richards may have been lucky that Goodall did not report him for abusive language, although the New Zealand team manager reported him to the Cricket Council for conduct unbecoming – but the issue was allowed to die. The whole of New Zealand was outraged but this was kept in bounds by a replay which showed that, by a considerable stretch of the imagination, it was possible to make a case for Goodall not giving Crowe out on the first occasion; on the second time there was not so much doubt.

After that, we all moved to Christchurch for the Third Test where New Zealand needed only just over three days to return the compliment to the West Indies. The West Indian fast bowlers did not pitch the ball up on a greenish surface; Hadlee did. The West Indian batsmen played as if they knew they had won the series and were doing little more than go through the motions. Theirs was a most disappointing performance and was further evidence that all was not well with the side, although they went on to win the one-day series easily enough.

Before I left New Zealand for Honolulu and home, I relaunched my tennis career on Geoff and Pip Lindberg's splendid court in Remuera in Auckland; I had also acquired an impressive taste for those delicious dry white wines made by Matawhero – and I challenge anyone to drink a bottle and pronounce it right first time.

— 9 —
A Feudal Approach

Pakistan in England 1987: the charismatic figure of Imran
Khan • an already formidable side galvanized by his leadership • Karachi and Lahore power politics • David Constant
persona non grata with the tourists • umpiring
repercussions • Javed Miandad, Mudassar Nazar and the exotic
genius of Abdul Qadir • manager Haseeb Ahsan stirs the pot.

Pakistan's triumph in England in 1987 was very much Imran's. World
cricket possesses no greater patriot than Imran and he was fully restored
to health and bowling better than ever. Victory over England was now the
only consideration on what he had said would be his last Test series for
Pakistan. The memory of that ill-fated tour of Australia in 1983–84
undoubtedly made him more determined to win. I doubt if any captain of
Pakistan has been such an authoritative figure in the dressing-room
except, possibly, their very first captain of all, Abdul Hafeez Kardar.

Kardar showed many times later in his career as an administrator that he
is nothing if not a politician. More than anyone else he has lobbied for the
removal of the headquarters of the International Cricket Conference from
Lord's and, of course, he has suggested Karachi as the only viable
alternative. It was a reflection of his thinking and his continuing influence
that, when the umpiring troubles arose during England's tour of Pakistan
during 1987–88, the Pakistan Board immediately cabled the Boards of the
West Indies, India and Sri Lanka for their support. In this he was
undoubtedly supported by Haseeb Ahsan who, at that time, was the
permanent team manager of Pakistan and probably the most powerful
individual in Pakistan cricket.

In my view, Imran is not and has never been a political figure. His
uncomplicated objective is victory for Pakistan and the biggest disappointment of his career probably came in Lahore when Australia beat
Pakistan in the semi-final of the 1987 World Cup. He had planned the
final in Calcutta as his last game for Pakistan and the victory that he
expected then would, if a plebiscite had been held, have seen him elected
as the perpetual president of his country.

It did not go according to plan and, watching on television from
Bombay, I shall never forget the calm dignity and bemused sadness Imran

showed at the prize-giving afterwards. If Pakistan had won that semi-final and gone on to win the World Cup I wonder if Imran would have allowed himself to be persuaded to return to captain Pakistan in the West Indies. Haseeb Ahsan, on the other hand, was decidedly jumpy and seemed close to tears that afternoon in Lahore; maybe he saw what was becoming a marvellous way of life fast disappearing. At a subsequent purge of officialdom in Pakistan cricket, a month or two later after Mike Gatting's disastrous tour, Ahsan was one who went along with the president, General Safdar Butt, and the secretary, Ijaz Butt (no relation) and, eventually, Shakoor Rana, although of course, these things have a habit of changing.

The colossal impact that Imran had on his side was perfectly illustrated early in that Pakistan tour of England in 1987. He appeared to outsiders to be aloof from the rest of the team and, in their early matches against the counties, remained in London and trained at Lord's. Without him, the side was a mess and it seemed wrong for him not to be there to organize things off the field even if he was not feeling up to playing. As we have seen at the start of England's tour of Australia the year before, loss of confidence early in a tour need not necessarily be disastrous but it is taking a gamble to allow fortunes to fall to the level of Pakistan's when they were beaten by an innings by a Kent side which was, itself, none too impressive. It looked as if Imran might have miscalculated. Even the confidence of their already voluble manager seemed no more than skin deep.

The touring party moved to Chelmsford to play Essex, the previous year's county champions. A gleaming BMW decanted Imran at the back of the pavilion and we were eager to see the effect of those much-publicized nets and training sessions at Lord's. We did not have long to wait. Essex batted, Imran marked out his run, having already made his team look sharper simply by leading them onto the field. Now, in half-a-dozen overs, he transformed the tour. He dismissed both the Essex openers, including Graham Gooch, and the side around him looked like an orchestra which has moved from the village hall to the Royal Albert Hall. With Imran waving the baton the change was astonishing. Where the day before in Canterbury they had been listless, unprepared to fight, shabby in the field, no better with the bat and too ready to accept the inevitable, they were now sharp, athletic, efficient and irresistible. Essex were swept aside, Pakistan winning by 210 runs, and I cannot remember another side being transformed so completely and so suddenly in the space of twenty-four hours – not even England's in that First Test in Brisbane.

The first and most important single feature about Imran's captaincy is that he has the complete and absolute respect of his players as a captain, as a player and as a man. They are a disparate bunch, riven at times by personal prejudice, perhaps even by a desire to see a colleague fail more than to see victory at the end of the match, and, so often, one has had the impression that if the Pakistanis could play together as a side and put all personal squabbles and differences behind them their record over the years would have been so much better.

Imran was the first captain to create a unified atmosphere and to make all players concentrate on the larger objective. He succeeded where, in recent years, Javed Miandad, Zaheer Abbas, his cousin Majid Khan, Wasim Bari, Intikab Alam, Mushtaq Mohammad and others had failed. Imran looks a leader, he has distanced himself from his players – so important in a captain – he comes to them not so much as the chap whose tape deck they all gathered round the night before but, rather, as the more remote figure, perhaps as the old-fashioned pre-war amateur captain. When Imran did not play in these early county matches, he knew what he was doing.

When Pakistan are in the field it takes about ninety seconds to realize that Imran is the captain. He knows exactly what he is doing but he is more than prepared to consult his players; he listens to their views and then makes up his own mind. He is never panicked into action and, at all times, remains (outwardly at any rate) in calm control, in contrast, for example, with Javed who, when things go wrong, is obviously angry and, at other times, has equally obviously run out of ideas. The majority of Pakistan players tend to be a trifle highly strung and a calm, authoritative figure in control is important just as it is with the West Indies.

Imran is a clear thinker about the game, he analyses his opponents, he passes on his knowledge and tries to help his colleagues produce their best. There are times on the field of play when stupid cricket annoys him but he will not show it. He will never make a fool of a colleague in public. At all times he supports his players and yet he does not make a demonstrative fuss. He accepts umpires' decisions without acting in a manner that will irritate the crowd. It is not surprising that his players are in awe of him. Perhaps the greatest accolade came from Javed during the tour of England in 1987 when he said that Imran must not be allowed to retire and spoke of the damage it would do to Pakistan cricket – and this from the man who was bound to be his successor.

While Imran has turned his side into the unit most likely to succeed the West Indies as the best side in the world, there is also a more seamy aspect of Pakistan cricket. Imran champions his young players as all good captains should, but he appears to allow them on occasions to push the Laws to the limit and sometimes beyond. During the Leeds Test Match in 1987 (which Pakistan won) the wicket-keeper, Salim Yousuf, who is more than usually competitive, went for a difficult diving catch behind the wicket off Ian Botham, clearly dropped the ball but then picked it up and claimed the catch. Javed, at first slip, was in the best position to see and also claimed the catch. Umpire Shepherd was another acutely aware of what had happened and Botham then turned round and had a thing or two to say to Salim. Shepherd told them to cut it out and the game continued. Imran did not appear to become involved and, yet, surely something must have been said in the pavilion afterwards. It was all so blatant, yet maybe Imran takes the view that it is nothing more than excessive enthusiasm which must not be restrained – or maybe he spoke quietly and undemonstrably. It cannot help but leave a nasty taste if a man of Imran's calibre appears to condone such things.

Imran's patrician good looks, combined with a certain aristocratic arrogance, his height, his easy, relaxed, almost disdainful way of living his life combined, of course, with a matter of more than 300 Test wickets, marks him as a thoroughbred in more ways than one. These attributes mark him, too, as a natural leader. On the field Imran is a commanding presence. It says much about the perversity of Pakistan's cricket authorities that he spent so many years playing under the captaincy of other Pakistanis whose knowledge of the game, its subtleties and also of human nature was a good deal less than his own. He was hampered for a long time, too, by a stress fracture to his left shin which almost certainly prevented him from becoming Test cricket's leading wicket-taker of all time. In 1983–84, as we have seen, he took Pakistan to Australia for their first series of five Test Matches in that country. Imran was not only unable to bowl in any of the matches, he also became the victim of unpleasant intrigue at home and the official captaincy was passed over during the tour to Zaheer Abbas who was originally Imran's deputy.

On his day there was no finer batsman in the world than Zaheer. As a captain he did not have Imran's stature, as a man he was not in the same league either and he allowed himself to be used too easily by the unscrupulous at home. On this occasion he became the focal point in Australia for the supporters of Karachi in their ongoing battle with their fellow countrymen from Lahore. Imran, who comes from Lahore, played the last two Tests of the series in Australia as a batsman and this was the start of his emergence as the genuine Test all-rounder he should always have been.

Imran's great strength as captain of Pakistan has been his ability to transcend all petty jealousies, rivalries and intrigues. He is passionately proud of his country and his main objective on the cricket field has always been to win Test Matches for Pakistan. If Imran had not retired after the 1987 World Cup and stayed on to captain Pakistan against England I am sure that the problems involving umpires would never have reached the levels they did. Imran would have stepped in, taken control and restored sanity. Javed Miandad, his successor, was happy to stand by, watch and whenever possible to stir it up himself. I was not in Pakistan on that tour, but so many points of principle were raised that I have offered some thoughts on it later in the book.

It is fair to say that Imran has been the most dominant cricketer Pakistan has ever produced. The older he has got, the better he has become. At times, he seemed to approach the job of captaincy with the same attitude those portly Indian maharajahs brought to the job before the war. That could hardly be more of a false impression. His fitness is no less remarkable than his determination and at the time of writing – a few days after he took eleven wickets against the West Indies in the First Test in Georgetown – I would have no hesitation in naming him as the best cricketer in the world.

He is also a most romantic figure. There are many young ladies around the cricket-playing world who would agree with this. He has film-star good looks and has become the game's first sex symbol. Outwardly, he seems mildly irritated by this and finds it tiresome; inwardly, although I've never spoken to him about it, I would not be surprised if he enjoyed it. Supreme performers in most fields relish adulation, privately at any rate. Imran becomes genuinely irritated when questioned forever by lady columnists, who may have more than half a self-interested eye on a brief encounter, about the prospect of his having to return home to an arranged marriage as is the custom in Pakistan. It is a subject which has been done to death. Suffice to say that I have seen Imran as the most charming and courteous of escorts to some of the prettiest girls I can remember.

I have always found him the most delightful companion and as fascinating when he is discussing the broader issues of life as he is when talking about cricket. It is his example, his inspiration, his ability to weld eleven highly distinctive individuals into a unit and his fierce determination which have been the cause of Pakistan's recent triumph. I can well understand the President of the country, General Zia-ul-Haq, feeling it necessary to talk him out of retirement and into captaining the Pakistan side in the West Indies. It is always a great pleasure to bump into Imran in one of those bistros in Chelsea or Kensington.

It was ironical to say the least that, when he retired after the World Cup in India and Pakistan in 1987, England and Pakistan then embarked upon what was to become one of the most contentious Test series of all time. It was a situation which had its origins in the English summer of 1987 when Imran was still in charge. The Pakistanis had fallen foul of umpire David Constant on their tour of England in 1982. He had upset them with one or two decisions but, most of all, with his manner. Constant, who was never a great success as a cricketer although for a time he wore Kent and then Leicestershire colours, is an umpire who likes to be noticed. He is a short man who has developed a rather overbearing personality and can be extremely officious. The Pakistanis had not been happy with him in 1982 and the memory was very much alive.

When they arrived in England they let the Test and County Cricket Board know that they would not be happy if he was used in the forthcoming Test series. Complaints about umpires are almost invariably followed by outbursts of moral indignation. It is as though the honour and morality of the country itself have been doubted. In other words, the reaction is 'How dare they!' The media have a field day and everyone becomes full of self-righteous cant.

We're now running a little ahead of the story but events in England in 1987 and those in Pakistan later in the year were so inextricably entwined that they have to be dealt with together. The sequence of events in the Constant saga is not that important. He stood in a county match early in the Pakistan tour and then, when he was appointed to stand in two Test Matches, the Pakistani management protested on each occasion. The complaints would have been lodged before the names of the umpires were made public and, each time, the TCCB stood their ground and Constant was appointed. The Pakistanis, through Haseeb Ahsan, complained that Lord's had made public a complaint which had been confidential. The TCCB denied this and from the Pakistan manager's record of reverberating complaints it would not have been entirely surprising if, on purpose by mistake, he had himself let this particular piece of news slip. These circumstances only heightened the atmosphere of suspicion.

I believe the TCCB showed a remarkable lack of sensitivity and a surprising lack of foresight in not listening to Pakistan's complaints about Constant. It was Lombard Street to a china orange that England were going to complain about an umpire during their forthcoming three Test series in Pakistan – and what hope would they have of something being done about it if Pakistan's own complaint was not heeded now? I remember running into Peter Lush, then the marketing manager for the TCCB and later manager of the England side on that tour to Pakistan, in the passage outside his office at Lord's soon after the news had broken that the Board had rejected the Pakistani complaints about Constant. I asked Lush if he thought the decision might backfire on England during the tour in the winter. He told me he did not think they (the Pakistanis) would be so silly.

From the moment the TCCB refused to budge over Constant, events in Pakistan which culminated in Gatting wagging his finger at umpire Shakoor Rana could have been clearly foreseen. It is surprising that the English authorities allowed themselves to think otherwise. Although I was not in Pakistan I understand that the authorities made their case in a blatantly shameful way and Imran, who had retired, would have been the only man capable of defusing the situation.

The Pakistanis had a marvellous alibi in that they had, for some time, been advocating the appointment of neutral umpires; this suggestion had not found approval at the ICC and England had always been strongly opposed. Choosing incompetent or partisan umpires for England's tour may have seemed a good way of persuading Lord's to change its collective mind. The Pakistani umpires who had done such a good job in the World Cup were ignored. Shakil Khan, who was apparently a great personal friend of Haseeb Ahsan, stood in the First Test Match. Seven of Abdul Qadir's thirteen victims were out LBW and some of these were ludicrous decisions. Shakoor Rana who, as an umpire, has seldom confused any issue with good will, stood in the Second Test Match and we all know with what dreadful effect. I just wonder if, in the midst of their indignation at events in Pakistan, those members of the Test and County Cricket Board at Lord's who had allowed Constant's appointment to go ahead the previous summer felt the least pangs of guilt. They most certainly should have done.

Another central character in all of this was Haseeb Ahsan, the irrepressible Pakistan manager who himself played a few Test Matches for Pakistan in the late fifties and early sixties as an off spinner, although there was in the end doubt over the purity of his action. He has been closely involved with the fortunes of Pakistani cricket ever since and is a particularly close friend to that famous Pakistan batsman, Hanif Mohammad. Ahsan appears to be a genial buffoon but this could hardly be further from the case. He has an extremely sharp mind and a fair degree of cunning. From the moment he left the TCCB offices at Lord's in 1987, furious that Pakistan's complaints against umpire Constant had not persuaded the English officials to change their mind, the plight of England in Pakistan after the World Cup was probably being planned. There can be little doubt that he was at the time a powerful, if not the most powerful, figure in Pakistan cricket and it would be surprising if he was not, in large part, responsible for the events that took place in Pakistan late in 1987. As far as he was concerned, he had a personal vendetta to settle.

Imran was saddled with him in England in 1987 and must have realized that he could use his fearless and voluble manager to his own ends. I daresay he was happy on occasions when Ahsan sounded off for it took the spotlight away from him at the same time as making forcibly the point that Imran may have wanted to make himself. There were times I know when Imran felt his manager had gone too far but Ahsan seemed to enjoy stirring up Lord's as much as he could and wasted no opportunity to do so. For all that, as I have said before, Imran is the only person who could have controlled Ahsan.

One of the sad aspects of this business is that it has been allowed to cover up the merits of an extremely competent Pakistan side and it would be unfair not to give them credit for victory in successive series against England. While Imran has been the ring-master he has had some notable cricketers under him and has helped greatly in the development of the younger players who will one day take over.

Apart from Imran himself, the best player in the side has been Javed Miandad who, back in 1976–77, revealed an enormous talent when he scored 163 in his first Test Match against New Zealand. Since then he has been one of the most formidable and destructive batsmen in the world. His batting can be as reckless as his character. At times it seems to know no discipline, his improvisations are extraordinary and there have been few more exciting players.

He has never been the easiest player or captain for his cricketing opponents to get along with and there is something of the street-fighter mentality in Javed's make-up. He has always been an opportunist and many of his opponents do not have a good word to say about him. By all accounts, he was at his worst when captaining Pakistan against Gatting's Englishmen. Javed has never been a peace-maker. I daresay he has never failed to extract what has seemed to him to be the maximum political advantage out of any given situation. As we have seen, he can be none too scrupulous when dealing with opposing batsmen. It was Javed who ignored his agreement with Glamorgan and failed to turn up for the 1986 season; it was Javed who claimed Botham's wicket after Salim Yousuf had picked the ball off the ground at Leeds in 1987; it was Javed who made one inflammatory statement after another during Gatting's tour; it was Javed who made a quite brilliant 260 at the Oval in 1987. Maybe, if he lived differently, he would bat differently too.

Mudassar Nazar has become the old pro of the side. He is unassuming, modest to a point and a thoroughly efficient, undemonstrative cricketer who has contributed much more to Pakistan's success than his bare figures suggest. He has been a most reliable opening batsman, having formed one part of a fine opening partnership with Mohsin Khan. Since Mohsin's retirement, Mudassar has been used in different postions in the order. Usually, he has opened the batting in Test cricket and gone in lower down in the one-day games. He likes to take his time and is better suited to the needs of the longer drawn-out game, but his medium-paced seam bowling makes him an essential part of the Pakistan one-day side. His bowling looks innocuous although he finds enough movement to disconcert the unwary and usually bowls his ration of overs for a modest cost. He is the most charming and friendly of men with a lovely open smile. With Mudassar you see what you get. When he is watching a Test Match in England and Pakistan is not involved – he plays league cricket in the North of England – Mudassar is always one of the first to come up to the commentary box and say hello.

If there is another excellent reason why General Zia-ul-Haq was right to persuade Imran out of his brief retirement it is that he is the only Pakistan captain who has been able successfully, for the most part, to cope with that mercurial leg spinner, Abdul Qadir. Qadir is a most intriguing chap. He is a brilliant leg spinner, with a bubbly exuberant temperament which occasionally lets him down. He is a marvellous cricketer to watch for not only does he display the art of leg-spin bowling in all its true magnificence but he also shows it to be an art form which is, above all, supremely entertaining. I have not the smallest doubt that that arch humorist among leg spinners, the Australian Arthur Mailey, would have laughed aloud while watching Qadir bowl. On other occasions he would have just as surely wrung his hands in frustration.

You see Qadir mischievously spin himself a catch from right hand to left just as he starts his run-up. The ball is transferred back and then it is jump, jump, bounce, bounce, a compelling windmill twirl of the arms, the right arm past the ear, the hand above the curly tousled hair, then a stride and a half down the pitch. In his follow-through, if Qadir senses victory, that right arm twirls over again in an unscheduled celebration salute. In those few seconds are encapsulated the whole joyous art of leg spin as well as the glorious unpredictability of Qadir himself. Qadir's mercurial temperament probably prevents him from getting the best out of himself. If it had not been for Imran's influence I doubt if he would have been as successful as he has.

Qadir is like a piece of quicksilver and as difficult to organize. He is tantalizingly talented, finds it impossibly hard to listen to advice and is the victim of his own bottomless reservoir of enthusiasm. But Imran has been able to rope him in. He does not react to his tantrums, he tells Qadir what he wants and conducts a serious debate with his leg spinner and, when his arms are waving in protest or high emotion or both, Imran manages to calm him down. At other times, he ignores him. In fact, he quietly lets Qadir know who is the boss and Pakistan cricket has been the beneficiary. Both Imran and Qadir come from Lahore which may make it easier for both of them.

Qadir bowling at his best is a threat to any side in the world and he has struck an enormous and important blow for the art of leg spin at a time when it has seemed to be in danger of disappearing altogether. While Imran captains Pakistan the right climate will be there for Qadir to be at his best. Too many of Imran's predecessors have seemed to be at loggerheads with one of their most important assets. Imran, as a captain, has also been able to rationalize Qadir's bowling. Other captains have obviously relied too heavily on him. They have thrown him the ball and just sat back and waited. Imran uses Qadir as one prong of his attack. There are occasions when he should bowl and occasions when he should not. He does not demand too much from his little leg spinner and he realizes the importance of looking after him. There is no doubt that Imran's tall, aristocratic presence and his approach which outwardly at any rate can be slightly detached enable him to handle one or two tricky customers as skilfully as he does.

No captain could talk more enthusiastically about his young players, sometimes with obviously exaggerated claims; it is, however, no bad thing if a twenty-one-year-old comes into the side, obviously in awe of

Imran, and then reads or hears how highly his captain rates him. I cannot count the number of times I have heard Imran say, in those measured tones which have half the female population of the world clinging to the rafters, 'He is a very good bowler, you know.' Then, with conviction, he will justify it. It is far from being simple hype for Imran is a shrewd judge of a young player. At the start of Wasim Akram's career, Imran saw something which many others failed to see. He has always been a staunch champion of seam bowler Salim Jaffer and wicket-keeper Salim Yousuf is another of his protégés. He will seldom criticize any of his players – in public at any rate – and, when arriving in England in 1987 after a rare victory in a series in India, said that he had never seen a Pakistan side fight like this one.

The three young players I have already mentioned backed up Imran's judgement although Jaffer was most unlucky with injuries in England. Salim Malik, a felicitous stroke maker with a wonderful talent still to be fully fulfilled, Rameez Raja, brother of Wasim Raja, Ijaz Ahmed and Mohsin Kamal all left England at the end of the 1987 tour having made important contributions to Pakistan's success. They were by then better players, as were the players who returned to Pakistan from the Caribbean in May 1988 after drawing that series with the West Indies. Imran's academy of cricket in Pakistan may be lucky to have so much raw talent at its disposal but the boss certainly knows how to make the most of it.

As it was, Ijaz Butt, then secretary of the Board of Control in Pakistan, was a fellow traveller with Haseeb Ahsan and it would have suited them both that Javed was Imran's successor as captain. It is interesting that, since the England tour, these two and Javed Miandad have been replaced and it is reasonable to conjecture that Imran would have insisted on the replacement of Ahsan and Butt if he was to come back and captain the side in the West Indies. For the record, Javed resigned in order to be able to concentrate on his batting.

— 10 —

A Joyful Jamboree

World Cup 1987: a night in Delhi • key players in Australia's
surprise World Cup victory • India make a hash of their semi-
final • Gavaskar's stroke-play a sustained revelation • an
unforgettable innings for Zimbabwe • Maninder a reminder of
Bedi.

Getting to India in time for the start of the World Cup early in October
1987 presented quite a problem. The English season had ended only two
weeks earlier, I had just bought a flat in London and had a job to get it
organized before I left. I was going to watch the Group A matches in
India, leaving the number one correspondents to look after England in
Group B in Pakistan, and I had to be in Madras on 8 October where India
were playing Australia the following day. I twice postponed my departure
from England and finally flew out of Heathrow for Delhi on 7 October by
kind permission of Air India. The builders had finished the day before,
the curtains were hung, the fridge was going and the beds were made by
the time I fled for Heathrow.

We took off at 9.45 in the morning and the caviar on the flight was
excellent. The browsing and sluicing in general could not have been
faulted and we arrived in Delhi at the appointed hour just before
midnight. I was through immigration and customs in thirty-five minutes
flat, some sort of record. I had brought with me two litre bottles of Scotch
and, when I walked through the green nothing-to-declare channel, a
customs chap stepped forward and asked me if I had anything to declare.
'Yes,' I told him, 'two enormous bottles of Scotch whisky, one of which I
am giving to Mr Kapil Dev.' We both laughed and he waved me through.
As I could not fly on to Madras that night, Air India had arranged for me
to stay at the nearby Centaur Hotel. My next-door neighbour on the
flight was similarly placed, although he was making for Calcutta, and we
were shown to an empty bus which we were told would take us to our
hotel. We humped our bags in and sat down and waited.

In time, the crew who had flown us from London gathered outside the
bus and a steward came in and told us we could not travel on that
particular bus which was for the crew. They were also going to the
Centaur Hotel but we refused to budge. An impasse developed. We had

been sitting in the bus for forty minutes, we were tired and reluctant to move, and it was a long time before the crew was prepared to enter the same bus. They clearly regarded us as carriers of most infectious diseases for they gave us a very wide berth. Of course, it was the union rules that forced them to do this. As far as we were concerned, at least they were in and all seemed well, but then the situation deteriorated rapidly.

The driver came into the bus, took our cases out and deposited them on the road. To stay where we were might have been noble but it seemed to me to be foolish to be separated from my main case on the first night of a period of about six months abroad. We looked at each other and then ignominiously followed our bags onto the pavement. We were then shown to another bus where, mercifully, we did not have to wait for too long. In the end I got to my room two and a half hours after clearing customs.

That evening, or early morning, had still not quite ended for, after a final drink with my new friend, I went to bed knowing that I had under three hours before getting up to catch a six o'clock flight to Madras. I had just nodded off when I was awoken by a thunderous hammering on the door. I swore, beneath my breath I hope, leapt out of bed and opened the door. There, I was confronted by one of the most enthusiastic porters I have ever seen in my life who was hell-bent on delivering me four suitcases I had never before seen and hoped passionately that I would never see again. He had two suitcases in my room before I realized what he was doing. I told him to desist but he didn't appear to get the gist of what I was saying. So I tried to put it another way with just a little success. I then picked up the two suitcases but met him at the door coming the other way with the other two cases. It was a memorable confrontation which I eventually managed to win but not, I'm ashamed to say, without raising my voice. He then apologized profusely and smiled so charmingly that, as I staggered back to bed never to sleep again, I felt decidedly guilty about the whole thing.

During the Lord's Test Match against Pakistan the previous June we had been visited in the BBC commentary box by our old friend, His Highness the Maharajah of Baroda, who had joined the *Test Match Special* team as the Indian expert on a tour of England in 1974. He was looking more than usually dapper and was in great form. We got him to the microphone and I eventually asked him about his latest literary pursuits. He had written a fascinating book about the palaces of India. He told me that he was now involved in writing a book about Indian ports. I asked him which vintages he personally recommended, but it then transpired that the subject was forts and not ports, an altogether more teetotal affair.

When we had finished with him, Trevor Bailey and I told him that we were coming to India for the World Cup and he very kindly said that he would look after our travel arrangements and hotels. We gave him our itineraries but, sadly, the Maharajah was struck down by some nasty virus and was unable to carry out his duties as our newly appointed travel agent. I had arrived in India, therefore, without any hotel bookings but, on reaching Madras, I knew that Trevor Bailey was staying at the Connemara Hotel and, accordingly, I instructed my taxi driver who eventually decanted me outside although he ripped me off something rotten. I knew a hundred rupees was way over the top for the trip and told him so when we were about a mile from the airport, whereupon he stopped the car and threatened to throw me out to the side of the road so I had no alternative but to fall in with his financial plans.

I soon found that there were no bookings for me in Madras or anywhere else. Mercifully, the charming front-office manager at the Connemara took pity on me and a room was found. Then, I ran into M.L. Jaisimha, the former Indian all-rounder who is now a Test selector, and he enlisted the help of the Indian team manager and told him to fix me rooms at all the other centres – a great piece of luck.

When the first match began at nine o'clock the following morning I had been in India for less than a day and a half but it had been a full day and a half. Arriving at a cricket match at 8.45 in the morning was an unusual experience but, in spite of internal disorders, Trevor Bailey was in sparkling form. Alas, owing to contractual difficulties we were not able to do a live commentary on the match back to London, although we watched one of the best games of the tournament with Australia being the eventual winners by just one run when Steve Waugh knocked Maninder Singh's off stump out of the ground with the last ball of the match but one. The only person I know who actually put money on Austalia at 14 to 1 to win the World Cup was Frances Edmonds, although this may not have been altogether unconnected with her arrival in Australia soon after the final was played to promote her latest and most amusing book about England's tour of Australia in 1986–87. Frances has a good nose for a worthwhile PR stint and, to her eternal credit, does it with style.

If Australia were the surprise of the competition, their success was a victory for hard work and logical planning. As we have seen, their cricket had been in a state of turmoil for too long. It had been some time since I had seen such a fit, determined and enthusiastic Australian side. The team spirit was marvellous and they were a happy outfit. The original selection had been one of the reasons for this because, at last, the disturbing element, the prima donnas, the incessant moaners and those who put themselves ahead of the side, had been left behind. Allan Border was more relaxed as captain than I had previously seen him and Bobby Simpson as cricket manager seemed to be finding the job easier now that some of the less satisfactory influences had almost disappeared. Another reason for success was their excellent manager, Alan Crompton, who brought a healthy but never irritating discipline to the side in contrast to one or two of his immediate predecessors who had brought none at all. Theirs was a well-run ship and, of course, this showed on the field of play.

Surprisingly, Border himself did not make many runs which was partly because Boon and Marsh gave the side consistently good starts and, with Jones batting well at No 3, Border did not often get to the crease when there were more than a handful of overs to go; for this reason, he had to start slogging right away.

Boon's form was one reason for Australia's success. He's on the short side, chunkily built with a bristling dark moustache, and he bats rather as he looks. After being dropped from the Australian side in 1986–87 he has become more of a dasher who is looking to hit the ball from the very first over. He is not an elegant stroke maker, short men seldom are, but he hits the ball uncompromisingly hard. He and Marsh were a formidable opening pair in their contrasting but complementary styles. Marsh, who is also short, is a more dogged performer although he has a lovely off drive. While Boon played most of the strokes early on, Marsh usually stayed to take control later and scored two 100s during the competition. One of the features of their opening stands was their excellent running between the wickets.

The only blemish was Boon's reluctance to depart from the wicket when the umpire gave him out. There were two incidents, both when Australia were playing India, the first coming in their opening match in Madras and the second later on in Delhi – this earned Boon a ticking-off from the management.

Another key player in this Australian side was Steve Waugh. He made important runs, coming in at No 6 towards the end of the innings, although I felt he should probably have been moved up one place in the order, and his bowling, especially in the later stages of the innings, was invaluable. He reacts well to pressure and, at medium pace, was able to pitch the ball up and bowl straight. By doing this he played a most important role in Australia's one-run victory over India in Madras. His accuracy was England's undoing right at the end of the final.

Craig McDermott also made a big contribution, taking eighteen wickets in the competition. He seemed to have gone a long way towards working out the problems which have plagued him since midway through the England tour in 1985. He had gone back to his long run-up and was extremely accurate. He is still too stiff in his approach but, while he is unlikely to go down as one of Australia's great fast bowlers, he will do a useful job for them for several years to come.

While these four players were the main contributors to Australia's victory, most of the others had their moments. Simon O'Donnell bowled a marvellous spell in the final in what could prove to be his final game of cricket. Soon after his return to Australia, doctors discovered that the lumps on his rib cage, which had been troubling him for some time, were a form of cancer. It seems so inexplicably cruel that someone who is so young and with such talent should be struck down in this way. He has, however, thrown himself into the deep-ray treatment prescribed for him and seems, at the moment, to be winning the battle. Mike Veletta, who came into the side halfway through the competition, batted splendidly in the semi-final in Lahore and then in the final; Tim May bowled his off-breaks tidily throughout, Border's left-arm spin was useful, Jones seldom failed with the bat, Bruce Reid and Andrew Zesers both bowled economically and the fielding and throwing were always brilliant in the best Australian tradition.

The side's greatest achievement was to go to Lahore and beat Pakistan in the semi-final. In the final they always had the beating of England when, after winning the toss, Boon and Marsh reached 50 in the first ten overs against some dreadful bowling by Small and DeFreitas. Victory in the World Cup ended a long period of little success for Australia and can only have done their cricket much good although, of course, one-day and five-day cricket are two very different games.

I stayed in India throughout with Group A which consisted of India, Australia, New Zealand and Zimbabwe. India, who won the World Cup in 1983, were the most talented side. They recovered well after losing that first match to Australia which they were, at one stage, winning with ease. The team went on to finish top of the Group but then made a dreadful mess of the semi-final against England in Bombay. The scenario there was very much the same as it had been in the opening match in Madras. Batting second with ten or so overs left they appeared to be winning the match with some comfort but, on both occasions, succeeded only in panicking and throwing the game away. Both times, Kapil Dev was partly responsible, especially in Bombay, and after the competition it was announced that he had been succeeded as captain of India by Dilip Vengsarkar for the series against the West Indies which followed immediately after the World Cup. Indian selectors are usually unforgiving after a defeat.

My own memories of India's cricket in the World Cup will always remain with Sunil Gavaskar. These were his last matches for India and, at the age of thirty-eight, he was batting better than ever. His innings of 188 in the MCC Bicentenary Match at Lord's was ample proof of this. That was a long, determined innings based on concentration and patience and motivated by an irresistible desire to score that 100 at Lord's which had always eluded him.

Now, he turned his attention to one-day cricket where he threw off the shackles imposed by Test cricket in such a way that it was a job even for his partner, Srikkanth, a notorious dasher, to keep up with him. He played his strokes with an evident relish from the very first ball and was responsible for some remarkable feats of fast scoring at the start of the innings. In that first match in Madras India needed 271 to beat Australia and Gavaskar played a perfect cameo of an innings. In the first over McDermott pitched a little short and Gavaskar drove him off the back foot to the straight boundary with a shot of emphatic authority. In McDermott's third over Gavaskar drove him through mid-wicket, square cut him, and then played a delayed cover drive behind square for three delicious fours. I have written above, when talking about Boon, that short men seldom make elegant batsmen. Gavaskar, like Rohan Kanhai, is a gleaming exception.

When Reid pitched short, he was square cut for 4 more and then Peter Taylor came on to bowl his off-breaks in the tenth over of the innings. He came gracefully up to the wicket to bowl his first ball to Gavaskar. He has a kangaroo-like leap which takes him into his delivery stride and then the ball came towards Gavaskar with a nice loop and was pitching on a length. With fast and meticulous footwork the great man came to meet it and, with a flowing arc of the bat, drove it far over mid-off for 4. To all intents and purposes Taylor's World Cup ended with this stroke and, if that was not bad enough, Gavaskar came down the pitch in Taylor's second over and, with legs astride, flat-batted him straight back over his head for a huge 6. It did not matter that the next ball ended up in long off's hands for, already, Taylor's confidence had gone. His five overs cost 46 runs, Gavaskar was out in the twelfth over for 37 with the score already 69, and he had hit six fours and one six. It had been an innings of rare brilliance.

Gavaskar's 61 against Australia in Delhi was magnificent by ordinary standards, but he reserved his best almost for the very end. India came to Nagpur for the last qualifying match in Group A knowing that, if they were to finish on top of the Group and avoid travelling to Lahore for a semi-final with Pakistan, they would not only have to beat New Zealand but would, at the same time, have to score their runs fast enough to beat Australia's overall run rate. New Zealand batted first and made 221 for nine in fifty overs; India knew that they had to score those runs in under forty-two overs if they were to achieve their objective.

Gavaskar and Srikkanth opened the batting, Gavaskar with a fever and a temperature of over 100; he proceeded to play another quite extra-ordinary innings. He set the tone for it in the sixth over against Chatfield when he faced the first four balls. First, he came onto the front foot and pulled him over mid-wicket for 6. The next ball was on a good length and, without any apparent effort, Gavaskar drove it straight back into the VIP box which was perched on top of the white wall which did duty as the sight screen. There was a fluttering of multi-coloured sarees as avoiding action was taken by the women and one or two turbans bobbed anxiously up and down. The next ball was driven over mid-off first bounce for 4 and, finally, Gavaskar tucked a full toss to square leg for yet another 4. Chatfield finished the over with the curious figures of 3–1–30–0. It was not long before Gavaskar was leaning in to good length balls from Watson and driving them between the bowler and mid-off for fours. He was hitting good length balls with complete safety to the boundary. Watson's immortal comment later was: 'It was just like bowling in the TV highlights.'

In spite of his fever no one would have been more aware than Gavaskar that he had never scored a 100 in a one-day international. That same ruthless determination we had seen at Lord's the previous August now reappeared. As he neared three figures exhaustion almost took over but even that could not shake his concentration. After a few exciting flourishes against Patel's off-spin, he took his time in the nineties and when, eventually, he pushed Morrison to mid-wicket for 2, his 100 had come in eighty-five balls with three sixes and ten fours. It was only four balls slower than the fastest 100 ever in the World Cup – scored by Clive Lloyd. Still Gavaskar would not give up and when Azharuddin deposited the first ball of the thirty-third over to mid-wicket for 4 to take India to 224 for one, he was 103 not out. Thanks to Gavaskar, India had scored the runs they needed to beat New Zealand with almost ten overs to spare. His innings in Madras and Nagpur were worth the hotel bills and the air fares on their own.

Another innings in this World Cup which I shall never forget was David Houghton's 141 at Hyderabad for Zimbabwe against New Zealand. Zimbabwe had caused a big surprise in England in 1983 when they had beaten Australia at Trent Bridge. Most of the same players were in the team – four years older – and, for the time being, the supply of younger players seemed to have dried up. They were unlikely to be quite the same force this time. In the opening match they kept New Zealand to 242 for seven, a score which will win more matches than it loses, and when, in the twenty-third over of their innings, Zimbabwe had lost their seventh wicket for 104, New Zealand's total seemed more than enough, even though Houghton was well past 50. From the moment he came in during the third over of the innings he was the only batsman, until later joined by Ian Butchart, to play with any confidence. He was soon coming down the wicket and driving Watson over mid-off, he improvised excitingly against the spinners and drove John Bracewell for two handsome sixes, the second bringing him to his 50 in sixty-two balls; but it did not look as if New Zealand were in any danger. When he pulled Patel for 6 he had made 80 out of 125 for seven and suddenly the game began to take on a different appearance.

At the other end, Butchart was in control and Houghton went on. A sweep for 4 off Boock brought him to his 100 from 107 balls and took the score to 156 for seven. By now, he had built up an almost irresistible momentum. Sixty-nine runs were needed from the last ten overs and New Zealand were looking understandably anxious. When he was 121

Houghton drove a full toss from Watson and was dropped by Chatfield at long-off and, with Butchart producing some fine drives of his own, the 200 arrived. Thirty-six were now needed from four overs, which was a tall order. Snedden ran in to bowl to Houghton. He swung the first ball to long leg for 4, the second went back in the air past the bowler for 2, a tremendous heave sent the third to the mid-wicket boundary, another heave deposited the fourth to the square-leg boundary and suddenly a Zimbabwean victory was a distinct possibility.

The fifth ball was well up to Houghton who drove it in the air over Martin Crowe at deep mid-on. Crowe turned round and chased towards the boundary as if his life depened upon it and somehow, at full stretch, got both hands to the ball and, as he fell headlong, held on to what was voted the catch of the competition.

The new batsman, Eddo Brandes, was run out from the last ball of the over when Butchart drove to mid-on and they hesitated over what was, in any case, an impossible single. This brought in Zimbabwe's captain, John Traicos, the last former South African Test cricketer still to be on the active list. Five singles came from Boock's next over, the forty-eighth. Seventeen were needed from the last two overs and it was Snedden to bowl. Four runs came from the first ball and then Snedden bowled Butchart a full toss which he swung over square leg for 6, reaching 50 at the same time. The last ball produced a single. The final over was to be bowled by left-arm spinner Boock and 6 runs were needed. The first ball produced a single to Butchart, the second a single to Traicos. Butchart could only push the third back to the bowler and he swung violently at the fourth and was hit on the pad. Panic took over and, with Butchart on the ground, Traicos came racing down the pitch and was easily run out as he tried to get back.

It was a sad end to a great game of cricket and, I daresay, the perfect result had to be a Zimbabwean victory. As it was, New Zealand won by three runs. Houghton had, however, played the greatest innings of its sort I have seen in one-day match. It was an innings which deserved victory.

Zimbabwe were never able to live up to that extraordinary start although they had a worthwhile chance of beating New Zealand in their return match in Calcutta but, at the crucial stage then, they were let down by their fielding. Houghton also never found the same form again. One of the joys of watching Zimbabwe was the off-spin of Traicos. So often, he came on to try to check the flow of runs when the new ball bowlers had been expensive. In this first game against New Zealand his figures were 10–1–27–1 and they speak for themselves. He knew exactly where to bowl and off his four-paced run and economical action he was always tidy.

It was sad that Zimbabwe did not make a greater impact on the competition and it looks as though their cricket may well go through a period of temporary decline. The young players are not coming through and, as yet, the Africans who have it in them to be such wonderful players (as the West Indies have shown) have not taken the game to their hearts and fulfilled what is a latent talent. One of the sadnesses for Zimbabwe is that Graeme Hick, surely the most talented young batsman in the world, has decided to qualify for England. Maybe his quickest way into Test cricket would have been to play for his home country and to have backed his own outstanding talent to gain Zimbabwe's election to Test Match status.

In some ways I felt it was New Zealand and not Zimbabwe who were the most disappointing side in Group A. Without Richard Hadlee, who was unavailable, they seemed all too easily to have resigned themselves to not getting through to the semi-finals; as a result, they played well below their potential. Martin Crowe did not score the runs he should have done and I felt all along that they were more interested in going home, picking up Hadlee and getting on with their tour of Australia. They should have made both India and Australia work far harder.

They were not an especially happy team and one of the problems appeared to be Glenn Turner, their cricket manager. He had done the job successfully for several years but, in India, it seemed to get too much for him and obviously his relationship with the players deteriorated as the World Cup went on. Perhaps he lived too much in a world of theory.

Thinking back over my own World Cup there are other memories that come flashing through my mind. Azharuddin's on-drive against Reid in the last over of the Indian innings in Delhi is one. The security at Delhi for that match when the entire Indian army seemed to be present, bristling with artillery, is another. The left-arm spin bowling of Maninder Singh deserves a mention. His dismissals in that same match in Delhi of Marsh, Jones and Border were a real delight. He should have won the man-of-the-match award, but adjudicators so often seem to favour batsmen and it went to Azharuddin who also picked up three wickets after Maninder had won the match for India. Maninder inevitably invites comparison with Bishen Bedi, not least because of the colourful patkas he wears. Maninder is fast developing into a worthy successor to Bedi too. I asked Gavaskar during the World Cup what had made Bedi so special. His answer was very simple: 'He would bowl six different balls an over.' When Maninder learns to use the full width of the crease and not to bowl every ball from so wide he will have even more variations to call upon and will be a better bowler as a result.

The most extraordinary result in the whole competition came in the semi-final in Lahore when Pakistan, who had been carrying all before them and looked certain to reach the final, lost to Australia by 18 runs. Australia won the toss. Boon and Marsh put on 73 in eighteen overs. Jones, Veletta and Waugh all made important contributions, with Waugh taking 18 crucial runs off Salim Jaffer in the last over of the innings. A score of 267 for eight was always going to be a problem for Pakistan. They made a bad start, too, losing three wickets for 38, but Javed and Imran then added 112 although they were never quite up with the required run rate. Imran got himself out at the start of the final charge and when, in the forty-fourth over, Javed was bowled, swinging at Reid, Pakistan's chances had gone and a dazed crowd watched as McDermott took the last three wickets. Australia won by 18 runs and the President of Pakistan presented the winner's cheque to the Australian captain.

Then, there was England's victory over India in the semi-final in Bombay. It was in so many ways as classic an example of panic as one could ever see and was very similar to India's performance when they were beaten by Australia in that opening match in Madras. On both occasions no one panicked more than Kapil Dev who, with his experience, should have known better. A brilliant 100 by Gooch, helped by Gatting, took England to 254 for six, a total which is neither quite one thing nor the other. There was much local gloom when DeFreitas knocked out Gavaskar's off-stump in the third over of the innings. The middle order batsmen and opener Srikkanth all made a start, but only Azharuddin passed 50. Whenever it began to look as if India were getting on top an unnecessary and wild stroke would cost another wicket. At 168 for four, with Kapil Dev and Azharuddin going well, India had the advantage. Gatting brought back Hemmings whose first three overs of off-spin had cost 27 runs, and stationed himself with great care at deep mid-wicket. Hemmings threw the ball up, Kapil Dev went for it and Gatting hugged the catch. Hemmings went on to take four for 21 in thirty-four balls and India were bowled out for 219 with four and a half overs remaining.

One curious postscript is that the organizers of the Reliance World Cup may have had a great piece of luck in that India and Pakistan did not play each other in the final. After Pakistan's defeat by Australia, the Hindus in Bombay and elsewhere taunted their Muslim neighbours and, when the next day England beat India, the same Muslims got their own back. A few people were killed, but it might so easily have happened on a much larger scale if these two sides had contested the final.

11

The Perfect Day

World Cup Final: the multi-faceted magnetism of
Calcutta • walking with the throng to Eden
Gardens • neutral umpires an asset • 90,000 Australian
supporters • new voices in the commentary box • Peter
Baxter to the rescue • DeFreitas almost pulls off an England
win • a triumph of organization and, for the ordinary Indian, a
starry occasion.

Calcutta has always been the most irresistible of Indian cities. It casts a spell over all who go there for any length of time. Down the years casual visitors have stayed on to become old Calcutta hands. There is an indefinable pull which no other Indian city can match, a pull which stares out of the pages of literature. Kipling was full of it. The most recent acclaim for a city, which represents an eternal paradox, comes from Alan Ross in his marvellous autobiography, *Blindfold Games*. He was born in Calcutta and lived there until he came to school in England at the age of nine. I wonder how many other birth-places could evoke such strong and detailed memories which have survived unblemished for more than half a century.

I must own up to having been to Calcutta only four times over twenty-five years and never for longer than ten days at a stretch. Maybe I am cheating. I have been told the answer and am working backwards. But briefly I shall state my case. From the moment I arrived at Dum Dum Airport early in 1964 and drove through scenes and smells which will never leave me, to the Great Eastern Hotel until the last time I took the return journey from the Grand Hotel on Chowringhee to Dum Dum early in the morning the day after the World Cup Final at Eden Gardens at the start of a laborious journey to Brisbane early in November 1987 (my last visit at the time of writing), Calcutta has infected me strongly with its magic.

I can see, as I write, the bearers asleep in the tiled corridor outside my room at the Great Eastern Hotel as I staggered back to bed late that first night in Calcutta. Unversed in these things, I tried to help a couple of them to their feet, thinking that they had met with some misadventure. The only misadventure they had met was with life itself, although they were doing better than many of their compatriots, and, after sundry grunts and scuffles, it dawned upon me that this was where they slept. Scraping together what few fragments of dignity I could, I stepped past them to my room. I shall never forget the first Eurasian singer I saw in Firpo's and, of course, I fell resoundingly in love with her although, as far as I can remember, we never exchanged a word. I shall always remember, too, on that same visit, a drive through the streets of Calcutta with my old friend, Santosh Reddy – we played together for Cambridge in 1959 – at the wheel of a supercharged, clapped-out Austin. He has since moved to Hyderabad – maybe at the behest of the traffic authorities! In its way, that drive was also unique.

I also recall the polo matches on the Maidan presided over by the amazingly beautiful Rajmata of Jaipur, the commentary intoned elegantly and most precisely by Pearson Surita, a notable cricket commentator in his day. We played golf and had drinks at Tollygunge where we were looked after by that David Niven look-alike, Bob Wright, and his wife. At the races at Alipore Pearson Surita was resplendent and alone in a box, wearing his MCC tie; there, everyone was sure they knew the answer to the next race but, in the end, picking the winner is no less hazardous than it is anywhere else in the world. I still have a yellow race card from my last visit and inside it are two betting slips which tell me that I enhanced the day and the fortunes of that well-known firm of bookmakers, Aroon and S.C.Ghosh.

There is Eden Gardens, now the most magnificent cricket ground on earth. In 1964 it was a patchwork of concrete terraces, bamboo poles and hessian covering. On that occasion, the wooden seats in the press box had been painted green on the morning of the match. One distinguished English cricket correspondent only discovered this when he got up some ten minutes after he had sat down to find parts of his trousers sticking to his seat. The Queen Victoria Memorial gleams down, the Courts of Justice sombrely survey the scene and, everywhere you look, you never see less than six million people.

The streets are like so many small, unruly tributaries, the pavements are teeming, sacred cattle wander about and there is a permanent cacophony of car horns. In Calcutta you soon find it is obligatory to drive with the thumb pressed to the horn. Countless thousands sleep each night on the streets, more live packed into hovels than Westerners would believe. The smells are strong and, strangely enough, soon become rather friendly. And now, tucked into one of those small streets behind Chowringhee is Mother Theresa's home for the sick and dying. A fleeting visit to see the shining faces of her Sisters is enough on its own to bring hope to a city which was the home of the Black Hole of Calcutta and, for many, has scarcely improved since.

Just briefly my mind flickers to the Calcutta Cricket Club, the Bengali

Club, the elderly and rather rotund gentleman who was a director of fifteen companies and professed to being very rich, and his large, toothy daughter. I went one morning to his office in the back streets; this was positively and eerily Dickensian. On a lower floor, droves of dark-suited workers filled ledgers with pens they dipped unenthusiastically and monotonously into ink-wells. Upstairs we were given food and then paid a visit to the resident priest who peered at us out of a raised box and intoned throughout in a sepulchral voice. Perhaps this was a rich man's way to Paradise – a rich man who did not like to spend a lot. Anyway, there was no divine intervention to help us that afternoon at the races at Alipore. And all this and more from what can only be described as the merest acquaintance with the city.

It was appropriate that the World Cup Final should have been played in Calcutta, although I suspect the reason was the size of Eden Gardens rather than any higher feelings for the city itself. Arriving from Bombay I found that the Grand Hotel was heavily overbooked but the sure hands of the convenor of the competition, Mr Inderjhit Bindra, worked wonders even if it was past one o'clock in the morning before a room was allotted to me. That done, some of us walked over the Maidan with Mr Bindra to Eden Gardens which is just ten minutes away. The lights were on, the ground was empty save for security wallahs and some cleaners. It was an unforgettable sight, not least for its stillness, its calm, its very emptiness and its serenity. I walked back certain in my own mind that we would see great deeds the day after tomorrow even though the finalists were Australia and England and not India and Pakistan.

I was up early when the great day arrived. Breakfast in my room was good, although it bore only a minimal relationship to the original order, but, on such a day, one could forgive anything. The hotel foyer was like Paddington station in the rush hour and a peep outside was almost frightening. A few officials cars were in the courtyard which was bristling with police brandishing lathi sticks and with soldiers carrying more deadly weapons. It only became unnerving when the courtyard funnelled into Chowringhee. There, the police were holding back about half the population of India and having a job at keeping their line. It was immediately clear that transport to Eden Gardens was out of the question and, even if it had been a possibility, there is no way we would have arrived at the ground before lunch. The only answer was to walk and I must honestly confess that, although crowds do not usually worry me, I was not keen to face up to this one on my own. I hesitated in the foyer and was delighted to run into an old friend, K.N. Prabhu, for long years the distinguished cricket correspondent of the *Times* of India, and together we decided to force a passage across the Maidan.

We pushed our way out of the courtyard and somehow scrambled across Chowringhee, under the wheels of buses and taxis, and arrived on the other side with our lives intact. The huge crowd pushed, eager for a glimpse of the courtyard, everyone shouted, the traffic police blew whistles, every driver within earshot had his hands on the horn and still some of the taxi drivers seemed hell-bent on breaking the record down Chowringhee. 'Prab' and I staggered across and I shall never know how I avoided one bus which was belching a particularly evil variety of black smoke from the noisy exhaust. In Everest terms we looked at each other on the other side as if we had made the South Col – but only just. We now started across the Maidan, picking our way as best we could as there was a fair amount of surface water lying around. Often we could not help ourselves from being forced in the general direction the crowd was following. The numbers were astonishing and once in the middle of a crowd moving in a different direction to the one you are aiming for yourself it is extremely difficult to go against the stream, and easy to understand why, in these circumstances, people panic. Temporary barriers did not help much, nor did police who were hopelessly confused by our media passes, but, eventually, we reached the back of the pavilion and I am sure that neither of us would have cared to make the journey again.

Discovering the press box, the commentary box and the whereabouts of the telex office took time, energy and considerable patience. You thought you had found your way from one to the other when, on the next attempt to make the journey, a formidable-looking soldier with a machine-gun barred the way in a manner which brooked no argument and you had to start all over again. I had to make the journey from the BBC commentary box to the telex office every hour to receive a call from Radio 2UE in Sydney. Our commentary box was small and, as usual in India, was fuller of engineers and friends than it was of commentators.

At last, I had a chance to look at the ground. I was there an hour and a half before the start and it was filling up fast. No matter that England were playing Australia, it was going to be nearly full. The whole ground was magnificent. The huge stands swept round the far side. There was a sweeping gap to our left where palms and other trees on the Maidan waved their branches in friendly salute. At the far end the top of the Courts of Justice peered down, but all round were bubbling, excited Indians.

Already the noise was threatening. In nearby boxes famous cricketers of the past, who had come specially for the occasion, stood chatting. Sundry players and managers looked knowingly at the pitch, others practised on the outfield, one Australian was hitting steepling catches to some of his team mates and Bobby Simpson, their cricket manager, was giving slip-catching practice. It was tense and nervous, just watching. Goodness knows what it must have been like to have been out there. The umpires were out in the middle too, an Indian and a Pakistani umpiring a game between England and Australia – a brotherhood of nations and what a triumph for cricket.

One successful innovation in the World Cup was the use of neutral umpires. This has long been a contentious subject; but it has been supported for many years by Pakistan and the irony is that the umpiring troubles in Pakistan, after the World Cup when England was on tour, may hasten its general acceptance. There may eventually be an international panel of the world's best umpires. In the World Cup itself there were few complaints about the umpiring. The great advantage of neutral umpires in the World Cup was that they seemed to stop the worst excesses of dissent when an appeal was either turned down or upheld. We did not, in addition, endlessly see close catchers leaping around and shouting in an attempt to unsettle an umpire. Nor did we see batsmen standing their ground and glaring at the adjudicator. It is true to say that, in this final, one scarcely noticed the two umpires – which is surely the way it always should be.

At Eden Gardens the noise dropped a fraction and then rose as Mike Gatting and Allan Border strolled out of the pavilion in their blazers for the toss. Old friends and old enemies – they must have been struck more than anyone by the marvellous and breathtaking incongruity of it all. Border won the toss and decided to bat and the crowd showed at once that it was on Australia's side. This was hardly surprising for Australia had knocked out Pakistan while England had had the temerity to stifle India's chances. Maybe, too, this represented a good chance to get one back at the British Raj, although it was hardly a day for settling historical grievances.

It was a good cricket match although, as so often happens in the one-day game, the closeness of the result was a little misleading. In the closing overs the Australians had to be sure the Englishmen did not find the boundaries; ones and twos were tolerated, almost encouraged, for they did not matter. Seven runs may have been the final margin, but I felt it might have been 30 as far as England were concerned. Australia deserved to win although, if the toss had gone the other way, England would probably have come first themselves. This is not meant as a criticism of the groundsmen for, if you win the toss on a good pitch in a one-day match, it naturally gives you the best chance. As it happened, Australia's score of 253 for seven was good but not decisive.

As usual, they were given an excellent start by David Boon and Geoff Marsh who put on 75 for the first wicket in eighteen overs. As we have seen, their opening partnership was the main feature of Australia's batting in the competition and, in this last match, it was appropriate that it should have been decisive. After that, Dean Jones and Allan Border made useful contributions but it was left to Mike Veletta, right at the end, to apply the finishing touches with some highly intelligent batting.

When England went in they never recovered from the shock of losing Tim Robinson, LBW to McDermott in the first over. Graham Gooch never got going, Bill Athey and Mike Gatting were not able to score fast enough and nor was Allan Lamb, bravely though he tried. There was never a stage when I felt England were actually winning the match. In all honesty, it was not quite as exciting as that 7-run margin of victory suggests.

It was a day, though, which left an extraordinary patchwork of memories behind, both on the field and off. The crowd of nearly 90,000 was consistently spectacular, the noise was deafening, and the atmosphere in our BBC commentary box was electric. These commentary boxes are the one aspect of the new streamlined Eden Gardens which have not been built on the grand scale. Our BBC box was on about four or five descending levels with the commentators at the bottom. Getting into, and out of, position was quite an adventure. We had the day's first casualty too, for Chris Martin-Jenkins arrived looking like a ghost and grew progressively worse as the day wore on. It was devotion to duty of the highest order that he stayed to the end to do all his various reports and interviews after the match.

As always, even though Brian Johnston was not with us, we had great fun in the box with Trevor Bailey, Peter Roebuck and Mike Selvey making their usual wise and sensible comments while Jack Bannister did a little bit of both and Peter Baxter, our producer, nobly rolled up his sleeves and helped out with the commentary when it became clear that Chris Martin-Jenkins was badly under the weather. Our commentary on Radio 3's *Test Match Special* was being taken by Radio New Zealand and in the eastern states of Australia where it was also the only source of information in the closing overs. Australia's Channel 9 had decided not to broadcast the whole match live which, in view of Australia's participation in the final, was one of the more surprising decisions. I daresay our commentary was heard in many other parts of the cricket-playing world.

The cricket began with a piece of spectacularly noisy agony for England. Gladstone Small opened the bowling with Philip DeFreitas, a job he had done with notable consistency and success in the one-day games in Australia a year earlier. Now, his nerve seemed to go which is an indication of the way in which pressure can get you on the big occasion – and there is none bigger in cricket than a World Cup Final. Two runs had come off DeFreitas's first over and Marsh began the second with a thumping square off a long hop from Small which raced away to the boundary. Two no-balls followed and the over produced 11 runs to the uproarious delight of 90,000 Indians.

Bad habits tend to become infectious and soon David Boon was hooking DeFreitas for four and then turning him off his legs for another later in the over. The Australian 50 arrived in only the tenth over with the ever pugnacious Boon scoring 29 to Marsh's 10; this left a sorry total of eleven extras at this early stage. Gatting turned to off spin and both batsmen now swept Eddie Hemmings for fours. Small's six overs cost 33 runs while DeFreitas, in spite of one maiden, went for 34 in his first six overs. Australia's start was so powerful that after ten overs they were looking at a final total of around 300. Marsh had played the perfect foil to Boon in the World Cup yet again.

When, in the eighteenth over of the final, Marsh lost his off stump to a leg cutter from Neil Foster, Australia already had 75 on the board. As often happens when five fielders are allowed in the deep after fifteen overs have been bowled, the early torrent of runs was checked. Even so, a score of 150 for one after thirty-six overs was useful enough. It was now that England bowled themselves back into the match. In the space of 17 runs Jones drove Hemmings to mid-wicket, McDermott, sent in to have a hit, had three and was yorked by Gooch, and Boon's effort ended when he swept at Hemmings and skied a catch to Downton running backwards towards fine leg.

The score of 168 for four in the fortieth over was by no means decisive, but Border and Veletta now put on 73 in the space of nine overs which swung the game back once more towards Australia. While Border swept and drove in his own thoroughly effective way, Veletta looked more like an electric hare as he darted up the pitch for impossibly quick singles, played the ball away off his legs and back over the bowler's head into the gaps. Veletta does not hit the ball that hard, but he places it so well which more than makes up for any lack of punch.

A final total of 253 for five would have left Australia reasonably contented after finding themselves 168 for four, although it would still have been disappointing after such a wonderful start.

The crowd's affection for Australia became more and more pronounced when England batted. The noise when Robinson played back and not forward to McDermott's fourth ball told the story. Robinson's selection, ahead of Chris Broad, was a debatable point. It is true that Broad had not been in good form in the lead-up matches but he has such a good temperament and loves the big occasion so much that he would have been a justifiable gamble. After Robinson's demise, Gooch and Athey added 65 in seventeen overs and then Athey and Gatting put on 69 but not fast enough. England fell increasingly and decisively behind the required run rate. The batsmen all got out trying to force the pace but Australia's bowling was always steady and backed up by brilliant fielding; together this exerted too much pressure on the Englishmen.

There was, towards the end, one brief and highly dramatic moment when it looked as if England might just snatch a remarkable victory. The required rate was up to almost 10 an over when, with seven wickets down and three overs remaining, Craig McDermott ran in to bowl to Philip

DeFreitas. The first four balls of the over produced 15 runs, a straight 6, two leg-side fours and a single. Suddenly the game was alive. If DeFreitas could mete out similar punishment to Steve Waugh in the penultimate over, it would all be over for Australia. Waugh, whose excellent bowling in the closing overs had been so important for them, pitched the ball up, DeFreitas drove and Bruce Reid in the deep behind the bowler judged the catch to perfection. Seventeen were needed from the final over and the batsmen continued to scamper runs to the very end but, after DeFreitas's dismissal, it was only of academic interest.

The crowd reacted to the final moment of victory almost as vigorously as the Australians themselves. The players remained in the middle and the two managers, Alan Crompton and Bobby Simpson, came out to join and congratulate the winners. The England players walked out in more sombre mood and were joined by all the officials, who had helped run the competition, and the officials of some of the other sides too. I well remember Haseeb Ahsan, Pakistan's irrepressible team manager, grinning and talking non-stop as the presentations took place and the man-of-the-match award found its resting place on David Boon's mantelpiece. Maybe Ahsan was enthusiastically contemplating the immediate future.

Throughout the long, hot day the sense of occasion had been enormous and where else in the world would 90,000 people pack into a ground to see a cricket match in which not a single home player was involved? Of course, it is true that the tickets would have been bought when it did not seem possible that there could be any other final than India versus Pakistan. Although they had to suffer the disappointment of seeing both India and Pakistan knocked out in the semi-finals, the crowd still came to cheer and to mark the day with their own infectious brand of whole-hearted enthusiasm. They not only came to cheer, they stayed to cheer. Seventy-five minutes after the game had ended this huge crowd remained cheering everyone and everything to the echo, especially the presentation of the trophy to Allan Border. When Border led his players round the ground on a lap of honour with the trophy held aloft, a blind man might have thought it was Kapil Dev and that the Indians had won. Then, all the former Test captains present at the final were driven round the boundary, each in his own car. That also caused much jubilation and the crowd still stayed to cheer no one in particular, unless groups of smiling administrators huddled in the middle of the ground were reason enough. On reflection I feel they were.

When India and Pakistan agreed jointly to host the World Cup there were many who were not prepared to give them a chance of doing it successfully. As it was, it worked better than anyone could have dared hope. In India they scarcely put a foot wrong, even if it did need the magic wand of the convenor, Mr I.S. Bindra, to sort out the many and pressing

Mike Gatting and John Emburey: those pukka sahib traditions still remain
intact

(*Left*) Abdul Qadir: the inscrutable East in every feature

(*Right*) John Emburey: captaincy? Well, it's six of one and half a dozen of
the other

The Sydney Opera House: Bicentennial Day, 26 January 1988

(*Left*) Bobby Simpson: a cricket manager's lot is not always a happy one

(*Right*) Ian Botham and Allan Border: all sweetness and light before
Queensland play South Australia

Shakoor Rana, Mike Gatting and Peter Lush: enough said

Michael Holding: a less than perfect conversion after an appeal has been turned down in New Zealand

The Valley of Peace: as it was fifty years ago and still is, in spirit, today

accommodation problems in Calcutta right at the very end. Mr Bindra, who became a great friend to many of us during the competition, must take much of the credit for the successful organization in India. A big man, under a formidable and always extremely colourful turban, nothing was ever too much trouble for him. I scarcely remember him except in high good humour. His delightful wife and his young son, surely the keenest young cricketer in India, were also very much part of those exciting five weeks. Mr Bindra's greatest achievement, if indeed it was his, was to organize two waiters dressed like generals in the Ruritanian army to mount the stairs and arrive in the press box at Chandigarh, Mr Bindra's home town, with trays full of glasses of delicious, frothing, ice-cold beer at 9.40 in the morning. Australia were playing New Zealand in front of a capacity crowd of 30,000. The only comparable miracle was wrought by the Governor of the Punjab when, at his residence that evening, he produced an inexhaustible supply of highly drinkable claret.

For reasons of pure chance, I did not venture north into Pakistan where, if anything, everything ran even more like clockwork. Obviously, it was a great public relations exercise for both countries which bore fruit in the most impressive manner. My last memory of Eden Gardens that incredible afternoon came as dusk was giving way to night. I was on a crack-of-dawn flight to Delhi and on to Singapore the next day and, as soon as I could get away, I set out back across the Maidan for the Grand Hotel. This time, Jack Bannister was my companion. Although there were millions of people still there, they were just standing around and our passage was easier.

We had gone only a few steps when the firework display, which was to signal the end of the competition, began behind us in Eden Gardens. As cluster after cluster of coloured stars burst in the heavens it was extraordinary to see the joy, the wonderment and the hope in all the faces we passed. They were upturned, looking back at Eden Gardens, following the fireworks and seeing something that none of them may have seen in their lives before. The next day most of them would have gone back to a humdrum existence in Calcutta, but this was their night and, if the looks on their faces were anything to go by, they will remember it for a very, very long time.

12

Sydney Harbour in Excelsis

Australia's Bicentenary 1988: aboard *Matilda 1* to greet the
armada • a glimpse of the most famous house in Sydney and a
moving fly-past • Australia fittingly defeat New Zealand • a
nightmare patch for Jeff Crowe – he sportingly disclaims a catch but
Dyer does the opposite • Sri Lanka bedevilled by domestic strife
and lack of competition • the Bicentenary Test
Match • Broad's peevish reaction to dismissals.

It was six minutes past eight on the morning of Tuesday, 26 January 1988,
Australia's 200th birthday. I had been walking for twenty-two minutes on
my way from Sydney's Sheraton Wentworth Hotel to Pier One, under
Harbour Bridge, to join a boat called, appropriately enough for the
occasion, *Matilda 1*. I arrived at a road junction and decided to turn right
down the hill. The only problem was that the road was blocked by a police
barrier. It never occurred to me that the enemy might be pedestrian traffic
as well. I began to pick my way through the barricade when a policeman
stepped out and told me pleasantly enough to go no further. I looked at
him, I hoped, pleadingly, and said, 'Can you possibly help me? I am a
visitor from England and I am trying to catch a boat from Pier One.' His
answer was indelibly Australian: 'Mate,' he said, 'there aren't any boats
going to fuckin' England from Pier One today.'

Australia had won the first two finals against New Zealand in the World
Series Cup and so the third back in Melbourne was unnecessary. As a
result, I found myself in Sydney for the great day. I had been asked by a
friend, Rob Hirst, who is the top, bottom and sides of Tuckers which,
among other things, imports wine, to join a party on their boat. It was a
special invitation for this was no ordinary jaunt round the harbour.

Matilda 1 catered admirably for more than 100 people and Tuckers had
sponsored one of the boats which, during the morning, was going to re-
enact the arrival of the first fleet – the boats were replicas of the original
fleet. They had all sailed out from England, crewed by volunteers, a
journey which had taken several months. The night before, 25 January,
they had prepared themselves for the great day in Botany Bay.

After a dinner at the Opera House to celebrate Tuckers' 150th birthday,
Rob and one or two others had driven to Botany Bay to join their boat, the

SS *Svanen*, which is registered in Canada. During a mostly sleepless night they had sailed towards the Heads of Sydney Harbour. Our plan was to sail out of the Heads, join the *Svanen* and come back with her to Darling Harbour where the first fleet was anchoring.

While still on dry land the day had already taken on an incredible atmosphere and a strong meaning. As I neared Pier One, the crowds were enormous. People wore clothes which varied between late-eighteenth-century and late-twentieth-century punk – with just about everything else in between. We waited half an hour for *Matilda 1* and, while the crowds were heavy on our side of the bridge, they were even denser on the other. Every open piece of ground was packed with people pressed together to have a good view of the original fleet when it came in under Harbour Bridge on its way to Darling Harbour. Small helicopters belonging to commercial television stations whirled around overhead, collecting pictures for the early news bulletins. Everywhere one looked there was a sea of chattering, smiling faces and thousands of children were beside themselves with excitement. The day was memorable even before we stepped on board.

The harbour itself was already full of boats of all shapes, sizes and descriptions. In time we stepped on board our admirably provisioned boat – the first drink was quick to appear. We set off, having waited as long as we decently could for latecomers, and, because the harbour was so crowded, it was impossible to make anything but modest progress. Everyone waved and cheered at almost everything they saw. People were constantly tapping me on the shoulder and saying 'Quick, look at that.'

We had one diversion. We were steering a course past the eastern suburbs and, before long, drew level with what was currently the most famous house in Sydney. Le Toison d'Or had been bought by Robert Sangster for his wife, Susan, once married to politician Andrew Peacock. It had subsequently been bought off Sangster by her next husband, New Zealander Frank Renouf, who suffered a good deal in the stock market crash of October 1987. Their marriage seemed to fall apart at the same time and the progress of their union, or dis-union, with quotes where possible, was splashed on the front page of every Australian paper as she left him, he locked her out, she got back with her daughter who followed him everywhere he went in the house, they both employed private eyes and it became almost a P.G. Wodehouse plot in real life. I can't remember whether they were apart or having a trial run together on Australia Day. When we drove past, Sir Frank was standing by his swimming pool on the water's edge in white shirt and shorts and with a tennis racket in hand which he vigorously waved to all and sundry. It was a house which was always being sold for between 10 or 20 million dollars and one could quite see why. Many of the other houses on that shore are almost as magnificent and stunningly opulent; personal helicopter pads abound.

On our journey the noise was considerable as honkers and hooters and anything capable of making a noise was blown or pressed. Time raced by and it must have been a good hour before we turned right through the Heads; how our young navigator managed was not the least miraculous aspect of the day. I don't know whether the sight in front of us or the sight behind us was the more incredible. In front of us lay the Tasman Sea – next stop New Zealand – which was packed with boats stretching out a good half-mile or more. The tall sails showed that we had the original fleet in position to sail in through the Heads. The water behind us, stretching away to Harbour Bridge a few miles away, was solid with boats and it was almost possible to imagine that one could have walked back to the bridge without getting one's feet wet. Everywhere you looked the spectacle took your breath away.

We were going even more slowly now and, finally, drew alongside the *Svanen*. We shouted greetings to those of the crew we knew and almost waved our arms out of their sockets. This went on for ages as we came slowly back through the Heads and aimed for the Bridge with the *Svanen* on our starboard side, I think, but I can never remember which is which. Our progress back was similar to all that had gone before except that the harbour was, by now, even fuller, more noisy and more exultant. We escorted the *Svanen* under the Bridge almost to Darling Harbour before turning back and sailing again in the direction of the Heads. We had just gone under the bridge on our way back when a new noise broke. From the direction of the Opera House the Vice-Regal Barge appeared with the Prince and Princess of Wales on board. She was dressed in the most striking turquoise outfit and they waved vigorously as they went across from Government House to Bob Hawke, the Prime Minister's official residence on the north shore for lunch.

After that, we had our own lunch washed down with some splendid wine while our captain took us on another tour of the eastern suburbs. We turned right into Elizabeth Bay and waved at Michael Parkinson who was having lunch with some friends on the balcony of his apartment. We were back in position in mid-harbour for the next treat later in the afternoon, a fly-past. Now, there is nothing which can be more antiseptic, impersonal and boring than a fly-past. This was different: it was the only fly-past which has ever moved me and which I have ever felt, however remotely, to be in any way involved with.

Coming down the harbour from the distant eastern suburbs flew, first of all, platoons of helicopters buzzing busily away. They were a generous and noisy aperitif, followed by the low growl of a succession of aircraft which must have been almost as old as Australia itself. In time, they gave way to the early jets and then to lashings of, presumably, the current Australian airforce. It all made a great spectacle and somehow seemed to set off the day to perfection.

When we put into Pier One at four o'clock I remember thinking that it was far too early. The crowds were prodigious and the walk back to the Sheraton Wentworth a trifle exhausting, for it seemed to be uphill most of the way. My day was not over yet, for I had been asked to a cocktail party-cum-buffet supper on the roof of the International Hotel to watch the fireworks which would set the seal on the event. It was another delicious occasion on which the food and wine matched the magnificent fireworks and that is saying something for someone who was trained on the 4 June fireworks at Eton. It made me think of Eton and then back to the night of the World Cup Final in Calcutta but when, as a final masterpiece, the Harbour Bridge was lit up comparisons ceased. One just whispered frantically to one's neighbours, whoever they were, 'Just look at that.' And nudged them too.

The Australian cricket season in 1987–88 was really a build-up to Australia Day. The new world champions were cheered wherever they went but, somehow, the season was a little bit of an anti-climax after the dramatic final in Calcutta. New Zealand were no longer the side they had been two years before, although Richard Hadlee was magnificent and Martin Crowe not far behind. Allan Border won the toss in the First Test Match in Brisbane and, effectively, the match with it. He put New Zealand in on a green pitch which had a fair amount of moisture just under the surface and the seam bowlers revelled in the conditions.

If Hadlee had been given first use of the pitch I have little doubt that he would have bowled out Australia for less than New Zealand's first innings score of 186. It was at Brisbane two years earlier that he had taken sixteen wickets in the match in similar conditions when, of course, New Zealand had won. Martin Crowe batted well for 67 in New Zealand's first innings but it was clear that the batting was nothing like as solid as it had been on that earlier tour. More than anyone, they missed the dependable if unglamorous John Reid at No 3 although, as this tour progressed, Andrew Jones came to fill his place admirably. The problem at the top of the order was not solved and, because of this, New Zealand did not get the best out of John Wright who now saw it as his job simply to preserve his wicket and guard against an early collapse. For a time, Martin Crowe was similarly affected and, if New Zealand's two best batsmen were not going to attempt to take the battle to the opposing bowlers, the side had little chance of prospering. In the first innings in Brisbane Wright batted for three hours for 38 while Crowe never attempted anything until, in the first innings, he suddenly decided to play a fierce square cut and then, in the second, a hook without getting over either ball; both strokes were hit in the air straight to a fielder.

When New Zealand bowled, Hadlee was not himself. He had had a fair workout in the matches leading up to the First Test Match and yet, on the day, he seemed to be straining for pace almost as if he had had too much bowling; his famous control was sadly awry. Danny Morrison, who is only twenty-one, bowled well in parts, showing that he is capable of genuine pace and looked a real prospect. It was interesting to note that Hadlee spent plenty of time guiding and advising him but, as the season went on in Australia and then New Zealand, Morrison did not appear to learn. He has an irritatingly long run, the first part of which is wasted as he runs for some way at no great pace directly behind the umpire before emerging and building up his pace in the last half of the run. Some fast bowlers who have run a long way, Peter Lever of Lancashire and England was a good example, have said that they needed all their run-up to balance themselves. It may be the same with Morrison although it is disappointing that, even with such a notable tutor as Hadlee, he has, so far, made little progress.

The Adelaide pitch, as it usually does, blunted both attacks after New Zealand had won the toss in the Second Test. By now, the appalling batting form of the New Zealand captain, Jeff Crowe, was turning into a crisis. He had taken over the captaincy from Jeremy Coney the year before and had started by scoring 100 in the First Test in Sri Lanka before that tour had had to be abandoned because of the political situation. In the World Cup in India he had scored scarcely a run and his sole source of income seemed to be from the square cut which he played from wide of the leg stump if need be. Now, he had made a bad start in Australia and in the Second Test bravely promoted himself to open with John Wright. It was a noble gesture which did not survive the first over for he pushed half forward to Bruce Reid and gave an easy catch to forward short leg.

This time, Wright batted fifty-three overs for 45 runs before normality was restored by Jones and Martin Crowe. Jones is not an eye-catching player. You suddenly look up at the score board though and find that he has made 60-odd runs and you are hard pressed to remember any of them. His concentration is limitless, his defence is tight and correct and he seldom wastes an opportunity to pick up runs. During a long innings of his one does not make a note of too many strokes. He drives nicely through the offside off both feet and he pulls, but he is predominantly a batsman who efficiently and unmemorably works the ball away into the gaps. At the other end Crowe batted well without being at his best but they took New Zealand to 485 for nine declared.

Border then made his first double century in Test cricket coming in when Australia were 29 for two after Hadlee had dismissed Boon and Jones in the same over. If Ian Smith had made a leg-side stumping against Border when he was 57 Australia might still have struggled. As it was, with his usual admirable determination, Border steered Australia away from yet another crisis and, in the course of his innings, he passed Sir Donald Bradman's aggregate of Test runs although Border had played in nearly twice as many Test Matches as the Don, Australia gained a first innings lead of 11 but, by then, four days had already been used up and the game meandered to a tame draw.

This was a game which produced one splendid incident although it is perhaps a sign of the times that one has to hold it up and show it off. Border had reached 65 when he on-drove an off-break from Dipak Patel uppishly towards mid-wicket. Jeff Crowe dived forward and to his left and seemed to catch the ball as he rolled over. Border was satisfied and started to walk to the pavilion and the umpires were happy too, but Crowe knew that as he had rolled over, he had dropped the ball and, as soon as he stood up, he recalled Border. It was a fine piece of sportsmanship and was to contrast rather sadly with an incident which was to happen in the following Test Match in Melbourne.

The Third Test was as good a game of cricket as one could wish to see. For five days the advantage continually swung from one side to the other and the last afternoon produced that unique excitement which comes only when a Test Match builds up in this extraordinary way after five days' furious endeavour. When the last ball had been bowled New Zealand were one wicket and Australia 17 runs short of a victory.

New Zealand had been put in to bat and John Wright who, with Jones in such good form, had trusted himself to play more strokes, made 99, Martin Crowe 82, and Jones another good 40 on the best Test pitch on the MCG for years. The new curator had done a great job and it does look now as if the quality of the Melbourne pitch is one serious problem which has been solved. McDermott and Whitney, who came out of the Lancashire League where he was playing for Fleetwood as a last-minute replacement in the Old Trafford Test in 1981, took five and four wickets respectively and New Zealand were out for 317.

Australia made a bad start, losing their first five wickets for 121 before Steve Waugh, Peter Sleep and Tony Dodemaide (playing his first Test Match) took them on the third day to 357 and a 40-run lead. Martin Crowe, who made 79, was the only New Zealander to play a sizeable innings when they batted again, although all the main batsmen contributed. Even though they were nine wickets down, New Zealand batted into the last day, wasting a total of thirteen minutes while the last wicket fell in the first over – time for which they would have been grateful in the evening.

In the New Zealand second innings Dodemaide – in his first Test – finished with the remarkable figures of six for 58 in 28.3 overs of seam bowling of just above medium pace. He had shown excellent control keeping the ball up to the bat and had been backed up by some good fielding, including Border's hundredth catch in Test cricket when Martin Crowe tried to run him to third man and was picked up at slip.

Australia were left to score 247 to win in 347 minutes on a pitch which held up well. They were given their customary good start by Boon and

Marsh although the Crowe brothers dropped slip catches from both openers. They had put on 45 when Marsh shuffled across his stumps to Hadlee and was caught by Bracewell at second slip. Dean Jones looked uneasy and Hadlee seemed on the point of devouring him yet again when he played forward to Chatfield and Martin Crowe picked him up right-handed at silly point. Boon and Border now took control and, while they were together, it seemed that Australia must win. They took the score to 103 with some lovely strokes when Boon, for no good reason, drove Morrison into cover point's hands. Veletta now made Border a good partner and another match-winning stand seemed to be developing when Border was out to a beauty from Hadlee. He played half forward to what was an outswinger to the left-hander which cut back and had him palpably LBW.

The tension was tremendous. Twenty-nine more were scored before Waugh played back to Chatfield and gave Patel a catch at forward short leg. Veletta now went on to the attack and lovely drives brought him two fours in an over from Bracewell. At 200 for five, with 42 needed, Australia looked to be winning the match, but at 209 Sleep played back to Hadlee and was LBW. In the next over Veletta swept at Bracewell and the ball flew off the top edge on to his forehead and bounced to Patel who held the catch, diving in from cover. Australia were 209 for seven. At 216, Greg Dyer played forward to Hadlee and was caught behind and Dodemaide was ninth out at 227, LBW pushing at Hadlee from the crease.

This was Hadlee's fifth wicket, the thirty-second time he had taken five or more Test wickets in an innings. It took his haul of Test wickets to 373 which left him level with Ian Botham. Somehow Mike Whitney survived the rest of that over and then Morrison bowled to McDermott. He brought one ball back from the off which hit McDermott on the pad and he looked plum LBW, but umpire Dick French thought otherwise. French had not had a particularly good match and maybe did not have the confidence to give McDermott out but I will swear to my dying day, as will many New Zealanders, that McDermott was out. Whitney then survived the last over from Hadlee and Australia escaped, somewhat fortunately, with a draw. It had been a truly wonderful game of cricket.

It was unfortunate that such a match should have contained one extremely controversial dismissal. In the New Zealand first innings on the first day Jones was out when he glanced at McDermott and Dyer, the wicket-keeper, dived across to his left and claimed the catch after he had rolled over. Somehow, it did not look right at the time and the replay showed clearly that, as he rolled over, he had dropped the ball and picked it up again before claiming the catch. Border and Boon from the slips supported Dyer's appeal although the replay left no doubt that it was not out. It was out of character for Dyer to have done this. This incident contrasted sadly with Jeff Crowe's reaction in Adelaide when he had recalled Border.

The World Series Cup followed immediately after the Third Test Match and was not, in all honesty, much of a competition. Sri Lanka had come across to make the third side and were to stay on and play their first Test Match on Australian soil, in Perth in February. After a dismal showing in the World Cup the Sri Lankan selectors had decided to get rid of the older members of the side who had been present since their introduction to Test cricket nearly eight years before. Duleep Mendis, the captain, was dropped, Roy Dias was left out, Asantha de Mel and Vinodhan John were others to be jettisoned. They picked a young side under the captaincy of Ranjan Madugalle. It was a calculated gamble and one which did not, unfortunately, come off.

All the countries which have come into Test cricket, since England and Australia started it all in 1877 in Melbourne, have found it hard going at the beginning. South Africa were the next to join, followed by the West Indies, New Zealand and India and, after partition in 1947, Pakistan. It was some time before any of these began to win Test Matches on a regular basis. The only way for a new Test-playing country to improve is for it to play more and more Test cricket so that its players grow attuned to the new standards.

At the moment, this presents greater problems with Sri Lanka than it has done with any other country. Sri Lanka's internal problems are the cause, because the violence of the Tamil Separatists is stopping other countries touring Sri Lanka for they feel, not unreasonably, that the safety of players cannot be guaranteed. This means that Sri Lanka are at the moment playing all their Test Matches away from home, which robs them of the chance to surprise opponents, as they have done in the past, on their own pitches. They are only playing two or three Test Matches a year, therefore, while all their opponents are playing ten or more. It is a tragedy for they have great natural talent and, given the opportunity, would in time surprise many people.

This was evident in Australia where the abundant natural talent of their young players was easy to see. But having so little experience at the top level they had not learned the disciplines with which natural talent must be tempered if it is to succeed. For example, batsmen had not learned how to play the big innings of more than 150 which are necessary to win Test Matches. Their bowlers, too, had not been taught how to bowl in the context of a five-day match. Concentration of both bowlers and batsmen broke too early. Their lack of experience and opportunity was shown up, too, in their fielding which varied from the very good to the downright sloppy. Of course, the Sri Lankans are also handicapped by the fact that they do not have a first-class domestic competition in their own country; this means, in effect, that their best players are not having to fight hard enough for runs and wickets. They badly need stiffer competition. For all that, the encouraging aspect of it, for the Sri Lankans, is that, given the chance to gain experience, they have the players who are good enough to win Test Matches.

I think there were many people in Australia who were hoping that the Sri Lankans would win a few matches and, early on in the World Series Cup, they played well enough to suggest that they might do so. As it was they won only one, beating New Zealand at the Bellerive Oval, the charming new ground in Hobart. Such players as Mahanama, Kuruppu, Gurusinghe, Labrooy, Tillerkaratne and Ramanayake will all make worthy successors to those who have made way for them – if they have the chance to gain the necessary experience.

Sri Lanka stayed on after the World Series Cup to play Australia in Perth and although some players performed well enough to suggest that, on another day, they could cause anyone problems, they were not nearly good enough to test Australia and lost early on the fourth day by an innings and 108 runs. It made a most disappointing end to the international season in Australia.

Immediately after the World Series Cup we had the cricketing event of the Australian season when England came to Sydney to play a Test Match which formed part of the Bicentennial celebrations. England had returned home for two weeks at Christmas after their disastrous tour of Pakistan and had then gone to New Zealand and played some warm-up matches before coming over to Sydney. The England players were obviously under a good deal of pressure, both in Australia and New Zealand, after all the umpiring and behavioural problems in Pakistan. There had been some sort of inquest while they were at home for Christmas and now it was as if they were under a good behaviour bond. They arrived in Sydney with the celebrations in full swing. There was a cricket ball in a marquee at the North Sydney Oval, a huge celebration dinner after the Test Match at the University and many other festivities in between. It was organized beautifully and even it if was not quite the occasion of the Centenary Test Match in Melbourne in 1977 it was still extremely impressive.

The match itself was a little bit of an anti-climax. Australia were confident of getting their own back for England's Ashes victory the year before. It never ceases to amaze me how Australians can allow themselves to be blown by the wind. The World Cup was a one-day competition and luck is an important ally if you are to win any one-day affair. After that, they had narrowly won a series against a not especially impressive New Zealand side and had then beaten New Zealand and Sri Lanka in another one-day competition. It was hardly overwhelming evidence to suggest that England would be thrashed and yet, as far as I could see, this is what most people expected. I daresay the England side were aware of this and the effect was to make them doubly determined not to be beaten. After winning the toss and deciding to bat, England did their best to shut Australia out of the match. Three dropped catches allowed England to score 221 for two on the first day with Chris Broad making his inevitable 100 – it was his fourth in Test Matches in Australia in just over fifteen months. Martyn Moxon and Tim Robinson also made useful contributions but, overall, England went too slowly. They were all out just before the end of the second day for 425 and were surely safe from defeat.

The second day left a nasty taste in the mouth for one extremely sad and unnecessary reason. Broad, who was 116 not out at the start, continued his innings as though determined to score 300 himself. He took no chances and had reached 139 when he faced Steve Waugh. The ball was short and lifted, Broad took it on the body and it rebounded into his stumps. His disgust at seeing this was such that, as he started on his way to the pavilion, he swung his bat hard and knocked out one of the stumps in anger. It was a shameful act which had no part in any game of cricket, let alone a celebration match. On his return to the pavilion Broad was properly fined £500 by the England manager who now took a different view of misbehaviour than he had in Pakistan. Maybe his mind had been concentrated on his return home for Christmas by those at Lord's.

It was an extraordinary action by a batsman who was responsible for one of the first incidents in Pakistan when, on being given out in the First Test Match, he took such an embarrassingly long time to leave the crease that his partner, Graham Gooch, had to come down the pitch and tell him to be on his way. Broad is a competitive character who is seldom willing to admit he is out. It is an admirable characteristic of a batsman not to want to be out but it ceases to be so if he is not prepared to accept that he is out when the umpire's finger goes up, whatever the circumstances. It was a most unfortunate incident. It was even more extraordinary that he should have put on another exhibition of open disagreement when he was given out LBW to Malcolm Marshall by umpire Ken Palmer during the Second Test against the West Indies at Lord's in 1988.

On the third day at the SCG Australia lost seven wickets for 164 and England's only chance to win now was to enforce the follow-on. This they did by kind permission of one of the more remarkable catches I have seen, by Neil Foster at mid-on, when Craig McDermott drove at Graham Dilley. It was a skier and, having misjudged it badly, he caught it two handed in the middle of a despairing dive. It did not do England much good though, for Australia now batted out the match without any difficulty against some strangely wayward bowling, especially by the two off-spinners, John Emburey and Eddie Hemmings, who between them failed to make use of a pitch which turned slowly.

Broad may not be everyone's favourite man but his batting ability is beyond doubt. He began his county career with Gloucestershire before he decided that, if he was going to catch the eye of the England selectors, he should move to a more fashionable county. He made this decision after a successful season with Gloucestershire in 1983 which he thought had gone unnoticed by the selectors; he then journeyed to Nottinghamshire. Nottinghamshire had, of course, attracted Clive Rice and Richard Hadlee and had a good chance of winning any of the competitions. Broad also found an excellent opening partner in Tim Robinson and they began to make a solid impact. The West Indies toured England in 1984 and Broad, who is a good player of fast bowling and was scoring plenty of runs for Nottinghamshire, now found himself opening the batting for England even sooner than he would have dared hope when he made his trip up the motorway to Trent Bridge. He played in four Test Matches against the West Indies and coped pretty well with his front-foot technique.

He then had an extraordinary piece of bad luck. After the five Test Matches against the West Indies, the Sri Lankans came over to play their first ever Test Match in England at Lord's. They made a big impact with Wettimuny and Mendis making a great many runs and their bowling, always likely to be their weakest part, coped well in spite of Allan Lamb's fourth Test Match 100 of the summer. Broad made 88 which was his highest Test score of the year but it had not been the most convincing of innings for he had struggled badly against the spinners, especially the leg spin of Somachandra de Silva. As a result, the selectors decided not to take him to India the following winter for they felt that spin was likely to be the main threat to the Englishman. They turned instead to Tim Robinson, Broad's county colleague, who had a successful tour. Robinson held his place against Australia in 1985 and again scored plenty of runs. It was natural, therefore, that he should be taken to the West Indies the following New Year and swiftly those fast bowlers made much of a fragile technique outside the off stump and Robinson's confidence was temporarily destroyed.

In 1986, Broad had another good season and was selected for the Australian tour of 1986–87. He has always been a front-foot player but now, after a poor start to the tour and an indifferent First Test as we have seen, he taught himself to play off the back foot. He scored 100s in each of the next three Test Matches, joining a small and select band who have hit three 100s in a series against Australia. He adapted himself so well to Australian conditions that I was sure that, if he had been taken to India in 1984–85, he would very soon have worked out an effective way of coping with the spin. He is a highly intelligent and single-minded cricketer with a streak of bloody-mindedness which helps to get the best out of him. Whether refusing to admit that you are ever out makes you a better batsman I rather doubt and it may not make you the best of companions in the dressing-room either. But I have no doubt that Broad will be one of the batsmen the fast bowlers will have to dig out when England next tours the West Indies.

— 13 —

Bottom of the Class

Bad manners 1987–88: Botham leads Queensland optimism for first ever Sheffield Shield title • that optimism fades as Botham brawls • smashing behaviour by Lillee • Botham dismissed by the Queensland Cricket Association • Broad, Gatting, Dilley and Qadir bring the game into disrepute • call for an ICC disciplinary committee and a panel of the world's top umpires.

During the England tour of Australia in 1986–87 Ian Botham made up his mind that he was going to return to Australia the following season to help Queensland win their first ever Sheffield Shield title. He went so far as to say that he would continue to come back to Queensland until they had won the title. At the same time he made it clear that he would not be going on tour again for England. By the time he returned to Queensland early the following November he had brought with him his own sponsorship deal which was worth a lot of money to Queensland. Carphone, the group which had sponsored Botham and Graham Dilley with Worcester-shire, had decided to begin operations in Australia – the sponsorship of Botham in Queensland was a good way of getting themselves known. It was a fanfare launch with Botham himself exuding confidence in the way that only he can. His hard-working agent, Tom Byron, who comes from Brisbane, had bought him a house and was hoping to set up many other local sponsorships which would help keep everyone concerned in the manner to which they were accustomed.

I flew from Calcutta, the day after the World Cup Final, to Brisbane in order to watch Queensland's first match of the season, against Victoria at the famous Gabba. Everything went according to plan. Queensland won easily and Botham hit 58 runs in what I can only describe as a vice-regal display of batting pyrotechnics which contained four sixes and seven fours. All, or at least almost all, Queensland hugged themselves and told themselves they were on to a winner. Those responsible for Botham looked knowingly at each other and said, 'I told you so.' The Shield was almost won. There were, however, one or two significant doubters who remained.

Queensland and Botham went from strength to strength. New South Wales were destroyed at Newcastle, although South Australia rather spoiled the party in Adelaide when they gained first innings points. In time, Tasmania, Western Australia and New South Wales were beaten at the Gabba and Queensland had won five of their first six matches. Their first objective was to finish on top of the table for then they would automatically host the final which is played against the runners-up. If the runners-up are to replace the side which finished on top they have to win the final outright. Western Australia were the side that Queensland feared the most and going to Perth for the final, and winning there, is always a great problem. As it was, Queensland seemed on course to finish on top and Botham had not, apparently, put a foot wrong apart from a reluctance to attend every state practice session, not a problem, maybe, while Queensland were winning.

Although South Australia were disposed of at the Gabba, things began to go wrong on the cricketing front after Christmas. The last three games were all played away from home against Western Australia, Tasmania and Victoria. In Perth, Western Australia won narrowly at the end of a marvellous game of cricket but Queensland still had to visit Tasmania for whom Dennis Lillee was starting a new career, while Western Australia had to play New South Wales at the Sydney Cricket Ground, an extremely difficult venue for a visiting side to gain maximum points. And indeed they lost. Tasmania, on the other hand, had not won a Shield match for two years but now, in Launceston, they were to put it across Queensland in no uncertain manner. This game was also the occasion when Botham and Lillee apparently caused damage to a dressing-room and to a school honours board hanging in the room, an incident I shall discuss later in the chapter. That defeat in Launceston deflated Queensland, past the point of no return. It now seemed unlikely that they would come back to finish on top.

The final round of matches took place in Perth where Western Australia entertained South Australia and in Melbourne where Victoria played Queensland. Western Australia won while Queensland were beaten and the Sheffield Shield Final was played in Perth, at the WACA ground, between Western Australia and Queensland. Incredibly, after winning five of their first six matches, Queensland had made a mess of it. In the first part of the season the more or less consistent success of the Queensland side would have kept Botham's enthusiasm going. He desperately wanted to win the Shield and was putting everything into his cricket and it was coming off. Now, although he was still working as hard, the results were not coming for him. This may have had an effect on him away from the field of play.

In any event, Botham's life was full as he rushed around the place making personal appearances and speeches, and appearing on several television chat shows throughout the country. In the few days before the final in Perth he went up to Darwin to relax when, I daresay, some would have liked to see him at the nets. That might have been a good PR exercise but, for a player of Botham's extraordinary talents who had been playing all season, net practice has always seemed to me to be irrelevant. It was more important that he should look after himself between matches.

He returned to Brisbane and caught the aeroplane with the rest of the side to Perth via Melbourne. According to the *Sydney Morning Herald*, some days later in a reconstruction of events that took place on that journey, there was trouble in a bar in the Ansett Terminal during the stopover at Tullamarine Airport in Melbourne. The *Sydney Morning Herald* stated that Botham went behind the bar to serve drinks and that the Federal Police, who preside over airports, were called, but that the flight for Perth had taken off before they arrived.

The details of the next incident have been much publicized. Apparently, Botham and his colleagues were playing a tape at the top of its voice and, eventually, Botham and Allan Border became involved in a loud and unpleasant argument which included some pretty flowery language. A passenger sitting in front of Botham was reported to have turned round in his seat and asked Botham to quieten down. Botham then apparently caught hold of his hair and shook him and, when another passenger told him to stop it, he in his turn was told if he did not shut up it would be his turn next. The passenger whose hair had been pulled made an official complaint and when the aeroplane landed the Federal Police were waiting and took Botham to the Police Station where he was charged on two counts and put in the cells until Dennis Lillee arrived to stand bail for him. Greg Ritchie, another Queensland player, was also charged on one count although his case was not to be heard for six months.

Botham appeared in court the day after Queensland had lost the final, pleaded guilty to both charges and was fined $800, whereupon he left court and, in one of the most extraordinary objections I have ever heard, turned on the press and accused them of reporting only what the prosecution had to say. As Botham had pleaded guilty to both charges, goodness knows what else he thought they should have reported. He also said in his defence that, if the other passengers had minded their own business, none of it would ever have happened, the implication being that whatever the noise and language used the other passengers should have sat back and enjoyed it. When things go wrong for Botham his natural reaction is to turn round and slate the press. If he reflected for a moment it might occur to him that the press have, in the past and especially on the tour of the West Indies in 1980–81 when he was captain of England, done double somersaults to protect him from the authorities.

Not surprisingly in the circumstances, Western Australia won the Shield final after their captain Graeme Wood led an inspired rearguard action in Western Australia's first innings. His was an innings which won him a place on Australia's tour to Pakistan later in 1988. With the police involved it was hardly the atmosphere the Queensland side would have wanted and it must have been very difficult for the players to keep their minds on the job in hand – namely, beating Western Australia. A summer which had begun with such high hopes at the Gabba back in November had ended in a sea of discontent on the western seaboard five months later and the man who had started out as a hero had finished as the villain of the piece.

Immediately after the final Botham flew to Switzerland to embark upon his much-publicized walk across the Alps with elephants when he retraced the steps of Hannibal in order to raise money for leukaemia research. Greg Ritchie went with him. Meanwhile, back in Australia, the various cricket committees were preparing to pass judgement on his antics, both in Launceston and on the flight to Perth. The Disciplinary Committee in Queensland, presided over by the former Test cricketer Ron Archer, fined him and cautioned him, saying that any repetition of the aeroplane behaviour would result in him taking a long holiday from Queensland cricket. The Australian Cricket Board Disciplinary Committee met next and fined both Botham and Lillee for their antics. The Test and County Cricket Board at Lord's had had an observer in court at Perth when Botham's case was heard and they decided eventually that, as Botham was under the jurisdiction of the Australian Cricket Board at the time, it was nothing to do with them and that he had already been punished for his offences.

The one remaining obstacle facing Botham, which was to prove the biggest, was the Queensland Cricket Association who had the power to terminate his contract. It was no secret that Greg Chappell, an increasingly powerful figure in both Queensland and Australian cricket, had not wanted Botham to come to Queensland in the first place and was unlikely to want him to continue. It appeared that Botham had also lost the support of Allan Border, judging by his statements after the aeroplane journey, and it looked as if it was going to be a close-run thing.

I don't think there is much doubt that, if Botham had at any stage been prepared to say sorry for what he had done and promise not to do it again, then he would have had an excellent chance of getting away with it. Since the aeroplane incident he had shown not the slightest humility as he blamed first the passenger in front of him for interfering and then the press for misleading the public. When he was told of his subsequent rebuke by Ron Archer and his fine by the Australian Cricket Board his answer was reported as being, 'I don't give a stuff' or something along those lines. This was an extraordinarily stupid comment if he sincerely wanted to go on playing for Queensland. He added that a fine of $5,000 was only about 'fifty quid at today's exchange rates'. That remark was unlikely to have made him new friends in Australia.

The Queensland Cricket Association met and Tom Byron was given the chance to speak to them on Botham's behalf. He came out of the room obviously optimistic, saying that he had been given a very fair hearing. An hour or two later, when told that the Queensland Cricket Association had decided unanimously to terminate Botham's contract, Byron admitted to being stunned. He must have misread the mood of the meeting. Botham, when informed of the decision in Switzerland just before the start of his walk, said simply, 'I've been stabbed in the back.' He went on to say that he had had trouble with the authorities all over the world but that this was the first time that he had been sent packing. They were both naive rejoinders.

The initial irony about Botham's sacking by Queensland was that it seemed to have been orchestrated by Greg Chappell, the man who ordered his brother, Trevor, to bowl the infamous underarm ball against Brian McKechnie of New Zealand in that one-day final between Australia and New Zealand at the Melbourne Cricket Ground in 1980–81. That is one thing which Botham would never have done in a hundred years. There is little doubt that Botham's dismissal by the Queensland Cricket Association cost him dear in terms of sponsorships lost but I suppose there is a certain rough justice when those who live by the sword eventually die by it.

It was only later that it became clear that Botham was a victim of a staggering piece of hypocrisy. Greg Chappell had been the leader of those who wanted to get rid of Botham and was almost certain to have been reluctant to have welcomed him in the first place, and eagerly seized upon the aeroplane incident. It was only later that Chappell was revealed in a truer light. First, there was a surprising announcement that he had severed all connections with the Queensland Cricket Association and the Australian Board of Control and in so doing had complained about antiquated administrators. This was soon followed by a stark story that he had apparently been leading a double life and of course the girl involved had revealed all. Chappell's sexual activities were laid bare for all to read about. It hardly left him in the ideal position from which to point an accusing finger from a moral standpoint at fisticuffs in an aeroplane. Neither incident was attractive, but Chappell was not the man to torpedo Botham.

It was another curious slant on Botham, however, that his walk across the Alps should have raised around three million pounds for leukaemia research. He is an extraordinary chap with Jekyll and Hyde sides to his character. One can only wait in fearful anticipation for the next incident for this has been the latest in a long line and there is nothing to suggest that we have come to the end.

While Botham perpetrated the biggest misdemeanour by a cricketer in the 1987–88 cricket season, it was not actually done on the field of play although there were enough unsavoury incidents that were. Chris Broad was guilty of two of them. He refused to leave the crease when given out in the First Test in Pakistan and then knocked over that stump in Sydney. There was Mike Gatting's much-photographed finger wagging at umpire Shakoor Rana in Faisalabad. Graham Dilley swore loudly and audibly in the First Test Match in Christchurch. Then there was the Botham/Lillee incident in the Launceston dressing-room and, finally, in the West Indies, Abdul Qadir unleashed a sensational left hook on a rude and noisy spectator during the Third Test Match between the West Indies and Pakistan in Barbados. It was quite a catalogue of misdemeanours. And, of course, those involving Gatting in England in 1988 were still to come.

How should these incidents and an ever-increasing list be viewed? Let's try to analyse each one. The England players would have known that the odds were stacked against them in Pakistan and they must have discussed this at length. They would have been told repeatedly not to over-react to provocation. Broad is an experienced cricketer and would have known the futility of standing his ground when given out, however unfair he may have considered the decision. There was nothing he could gain by standing there unless it was his unlikely intention to make the series increasingly unpleasant.

At the start of the English summer of 1988 Peter May, the chairman of the selectors, told a portion of the English cricketing press that they must distinguish between dissent and disappointment, as if they had not already done so without needing a schoolmasterly lecture about it. Micky Stewart later repeated this slightly naïve argument. It is worth pointing out that the spoilt-boy syndrome comes into this too. Gatting's incident quite properly made the bigge t news as his nerve was finally broken by another petty and infuriating interruption by an umpire who had almost certainly been sent there to do a job which took no account of the niceties of the game. No one should have been more aware than Gatting of the increasing indignities England were going to be made to suffer. At every team meeting every day before play the England players should have been saying to themselves, 'Do not react,' and no one more so than the captain. Whatever the injustice, whatever the provocation – and it was extreme – they could not justify Gatting's actions. I admit I was several thousand miles away in Australia at the time but it was surely the classical situation where you must turn again the other cheek and go on turning it. In any contest where there are adjudicators, their rule must be upheld and the worse or the more incompetent that rule becomes the more important it is that it should be upheld, otherwise chaos ensues.

The incident that finally sparked off Gatting's argument with Shakoor Rana was relatively minor, but it was obviously the last in a long succession of niggles. By behaving as he did, Gatting played completely into Pakistani hands and, in my view, he forfeited his right to captain England again. It was shameful that an England captain should have behaved like this. It was extraordinary to find, at the start of the English summer of 1988, that this particular slate appeared to have been wiped clean. It was, in the circumstances, unbelievable that the players should each have been given a bonus of £1000 on their return to England after the tour. It is easy to question the morality of that. Things have come to a pretty pass when an England captain can behave as Gatting did, and not only get away with it but also be given a reward. My mind goes back, once again, to Keith Fletcher flipping his bales off in India and the penalty he paid soon afterwards. Or does Gatting owe his retention – he was appointed to captain England in the three one-day internationals in the first two Test Matches against the West Indies in 1988 – to the fact that there was no obvious alternative?

It was not an especially pretty winter season for English cricket in 1987–88. Although Broad's and Gatting's contributions were the most noticeable, I have no doubt there were others and that, in Pakistan, the players were looking and waiting for anything that could be seen as an implied or actual insult. Life on the sub-continent can be difficult, especially for those who want to make it so. I can think of other captains who have taken tours there, such as Tony Lewis and Tony Greig, who, in their own ways, would have kept their sense of humour and tried to get one back on the umpires. They would never have reacted as Gatting did, however extreme the provocation. Gatting's behaviour was, to say the least, surprising.

Some of the subsequent reactions in support of Gatting by people who should have known better have been even more surprising. There can be little doubt that the captain and management of that tour were set up. It was extraordinary that they should have fallen for it. At least, unlike earlier touring sides, they were living mostly in four- and five-star hotels and it may be just another instance of how, when cricketers become spoilt, they lose their sense of humour. I doubt there are any circumstances in which such behaviour can be condoned. It is a comment on the age in which we live that such fundamental issues should even be open to discussion.

The next piece of bad behaviour came when Broad bashed his stumps down in Sydney. This is something which, at times, we may all have felt like doing but we have been prevented by the traditions of the game within which we have all been brought up. Cricket is a character-forming game. The phrase, 'it isn't cricket', is not just blimpish jingoistic nonsense but implies a certain basic decency. Knocking over your stumps has been unacceptable for hundreds of years at any level. Why now should a player do it in a Test Match? Is it a lack of personal discipline? Or is it simply a commentary on the times in which we live when anything goes? All these incidents show a basic lack of respect for the game, both for its unwritten code of conduct and for its Laws which are spelled out in *Wisden*. Broad, having been in trouble in Pakistan, surely should have been all too mindful of behaving himself in Sydney. He claims it all happened in the heat of the moment but Test cricketers' reflexes should be conditioned by the traditions of a game they have played for so long. Cricket ceases to be the game we know and love if the stage is reached when these things do not matter.

In New Zealand, Dilley had an appeal turned down and swore loudly and embarrassingly. I was told that the words he used could be heard clearly by spectators sitting in the stands. Because of the microphones fixed to the bottom of the stumps the television audience was left in no doubt either. I was amazed that the manager of the England side who, because he is involved in the commercial aspects of the game at Lord's and knows all too well about television contracts, should have tried to persuade the authorities concerned to have the microphones taken away. What about telling the players to put a sock in it? By asking for the microphones to be taken away it is almost as if he is condoning what was said, and what countless schoolchildren may have heard, and it is not as though modern players are not aware that there are microphones on the stumps. Dilley was fined £250 by the manager, which was a modest penalty. One of cricket's main problems these days is that the captain and the managers almost invariably end up as 'one of the boys' which makes it almost impossible for them to remain objective over disciplinary matters.

In March the Pakistan side with Imran back in charge, and Intikhab Alam restored as manager, I daresay at Imran's request for I cannot believe that he will have wanted to tour again with Haseeb Ahsan as his manager, toured the West Indies and drew a thrilling series one all. In the Third Test Match in Bridgetown an exciting finish was building up on the last day. It looked as if Pakistan would win when two wickets, including that of Viv Richards, went down early in the day but then Jeff Dujon and Winston Benjamin took the West Indies to victory with a remarkable ninth-wicket stand. During their partnership the leg spinner, Abdul Qadir, had two appeals turned down, which angered him, and when, after the second, he returned to field on the boundary he was the subject of a good deal of hostile comment from the crowd.

There was one young man in particular whom Qadir later said had been abusing him all day. Quite suddenly, Qadir could stand it no longer and strode over the boundary, into the crowd sitting in the open ground behind the rope, and punched the spectator with a choice left hook. The police quickly stepped in and one of the other fielders shepherded away a fuming Qadir. The Pakistanis said that Qadir wanted to press charges against the spectator but the case would not have been heard for some weeks. In the event, the Pakistani management paid the spectator a sum in excess of £500 which was hardly the action of people who were sure they were in the right.

Qadir is known for his excitable qualities but there can be no conceivable excuse or forgiveness for such an offence and yet, by the time Qadir arrived home in Lahore, he was greeted, I daresay, as a hero and no further action was apparently taken. I do not agree that he should be banned for life but I am sure that he should be made to atone for such wretched behaviour and a massive fine would be the best way of doing it. If Mr Haseeb Ahsan has created such feelings of invulnerability among his recent charges, he has more to answer for than I thought.

The one common denominator in all these incidents is that the governing bodies of the countries concerned are appearing, to ordinary people, to be running away from these incidents of bad behaviour. If not being justified, they are at least being ignored, publicly at any rate, when what is needed more than anything is for a public exhibition to be made of the culprits for, if that happens, there is a chance that others will be discouraged from acting in similar fashion. I think that these bodies are failing in another important duty, too, for these cricketers are hero-worshipped by countless thousands of small children. If their heroes are not publicly rebuked these children can be forgiven for thinking that such behaviour is respectable and can be imitated with impunity. Many people seem to be ignoring their responsibilities.

I believe that the time has come for an international disciplinary committee to be set up which should sit in judgement in cases of bad behaviour involving Test cricketers. Until such basic disciplines are seen to be insisted upon, the law of the jungle will increasingly take charge. Cricket is a game which demands and deserves respect and players who consider that ordinary civilized rules do not apply to them should be made to pay the penalty. I do not believe that the governing bodies of individual countries are prepared to face up to what is going on and that disciplinary powers should therefore be given to an outside body.

I am also sure that recent events have made it important that a body, not of neutral umpires (for all umpires should be neutral) but of the world's best umpires, should be set up and used for Test cricket everywhere. The umpiring has, in 1987–88 alone, caused problems all round the cricket-playing world. If there is a repeat of the situation which happened between England and Pakistan, cricketing relations between the two countries could be broken off for a long time to come. This would be extremely damaging and, to prevent the possibility of this happening, a panel of the world's best umpires is an urgent necessity. It is sad that this has to happen to a game which has lived for so long on the tradition that the players accept the umpire's word, but the time has come to act. It is going to be up to the ICC to throw off its reputation as a toothless tiger, to put its best foot forward to act for the common good and clean up the game so that, if such unsavoury incidents are repeated, the guilty should pay the price. If the ICC shirks this issue I fear for the future of cricket. The last twelve months have been an absolute disgrace. I rest my case.

— 14 —

A World Apart

The tour goes on 1987–88: New Zealand and England bring nothing
but boredom • the world awaits Hadlee's 374th Test
wicket • for John Wright captaincy at last • New Zealand's
newcomers • the Valley of Peace • a new English season
begins with Compton's seventieth birthday celebrations and the
ageless Dennis Lillee.

By the time I arrived in New Zealand, England had already drawn the
First Test Match at Christchurch for they were unable, because of the
weather, to push home an important advantage produced for them largely
by the splendid bowling of the voluble Graham Dilley and the batting of
Chris Broad who had hit yet another Test Match 100. This was the Test
Match when all Christchurch, his home town, were hoping that Richard
Hadlee would break the record for the largest number of Test wickets.
When the match began he and Ian Botham were both level on 373 but,
having bowled beautifully up until tea-time on the first day but without
success, he then pulled a muscle in his shin and was unable to bowl again in
the series. While bad luck plagued Hadlee, Dilley produced arguably the
best bowling of his England career although, as we have seen, he did much
to discount this by swearing when a couple of umpiring decisions did not
go his way in the New Zealand second innings. The Second and Third
Test Matches were also drawn on boring pitches. There were some good
individual performances, some strange umpiring decisions and a chance
for our old friend, umpire Fred Goodall, to strut around the stage, surely
for the last time.

These three Test Matches and the one-day series that followed were, in
one way, a considerable help to New Zealand cricket. Andrew Jones was
injured in the First Test Match and, as a result, the left-handed Mark
Greatbatch was thrust into the Second and looked the part as a middle-
order batsman scoring 100 in New Zealand's second innings. John Wright
had made 100 in the first and, in England's first innings, Martyn Moxon,
after batting extremely well, became marooned in the nineties before
being caught at first slip off Chatfield when one short of his 100. When a
batsman who is new to Test cricket fails so narrowly to make his first 100
it can leave a psychological blockage. Moxon's immediate position in the

England side is, of course, going to depend on Gooch's appetite for the game at this level.

The real dramas of the Second Test at Eden Park were enacted in the pavilion. As we have seen in India during the World Cup and then in Australia, Jeff Crowe's batting had disintegrated. Not only was he unable to score a run but he was beginning to look as if he had lost all idea of how to bat. In Australia he had left himself out of the side for one or two one-day internationals at the end and now, in New Zealand, it looked as if he would have to be dropped at the end of the series against England. But, in Auckland, the selectors decided that the time had come and Crowe was replaced by Wright and also dropped from the side for the Third Test in Wellington.

It was sad for Jeff Crowe for he is such a likeable and friendly chap but his form had been such that he could really have had no complaints. When he inherited the job from Jeremy Coney his first task was to take the side for a short series to Sri Lanka. They played one Test Match in which Crowe himself scored 100 before the tour was abandoned because of the activities of the Tamil Tigers. Jeff Crowe would almost certainly not have been given the job if John Wright had been available, but it was Wright's benefit season with Derbyshire and he had to return to England as soon as the West Indies series was over. Wright had wanted to captain New Zealand for some time but it had begun to look as if he would never get the chance. Then Jeff Crowe lost form and, suddenly, on the last evening of the Test against England Wright found that, at long last, he had the captaincy.

He won the toss in Wellington and batted but New Zealand made remarkably slow progress and had reached only 192 for three at the end of the first day. Martin Crowe made 100 after that, Greatbatch passed 60 and Ken Rutherford made a brilliant 91 not out by the end of the second day. If the New Zealand selectors had not so foolishly tried to use Rutherford as a makeshift opener for so long and had kept him at No 6, his rightful position, he would probably have already established himself as a Test batsman. In this Third Test he batted well enough to suggest that he would score a great many more runs for New Zealand. In order to allow him to complete his 100 Wright continued New Zealand's innings into the third day before declaring at 512 for six. With only just over two and a half days left England had no great problems in batting out the match to end one of the most boring series I can remember.

There followed four one-day games, the first two of which were won by England and the last two by New Zealand. They were not especially eventful although the New Zealanders brought in middle-order batsman and medium-paced seam bowler, Chris Kuggeleijn, who is of Dutch origin. He showed himself to be a pretty useful player and it will be interesting to see how he copes with Test cricket. In the Third Test of the series another newcomer, Robert Vance, son of the Chairman of the New Zealand Cricket Council, also played a promising innings and so, by the end of their season, New Zealand's batting prospects were brighter than had seemed likely. But they still have ahead of them the job of trying to replace Richard Hadlee.

For me, it had been a busy few months which had begun at the Chapauk Stadium in Madras on 9 October and had ended at Eden Park, Auckland, on 19 March. I had watched seventy-one days' cricket, spoken goodness knows how many words about the game and written a few more besides. One day's cricket I have not included in my overall total was, in some ways, the best of all.

During the Wellington Test Match I was asked by Ian Galloway, New Zealand's best and most experienced cricket commentator now that Alan Richards has retired, if I would like to visit the Valley of Peace Cricket Club. The Valley of Peace were playing a side from Otago. Ian told me it was a beautifully picturesque but tiny ground, ringed with enormous trees, deep in the country, where cricket had been played for more than fifty years; it was also a ground which no woman was allowed to set foot on. My views about male chauvinism in Australia are well known for I infinitely prefer the company of women to men, but this seemed too ridiculous and I thought I had better investigate.

As a result, I had one of the most enjoyable days I have ever spent at a cricket ground anywhere in the world. If the next few paragraphs read a little like a history book, so be it, for it is a story worth telling and a good note on which to end this book for somehow it puts all the pages before these few into a perspective we should never lose. Cricket is a game which has always been played for people to enjoy. If there were no Valleys of Peace in this world we would all be the poorer for it.

I was picked up at the Cotswold Motor Inn, an exceedingly comfortable hostelry where I always stay in Christchurch, by Alby Duckmanton who had just managed the New Zealand side in Australia. He drove me the ten miles or so to the ground which nestles at the front of the Cashmere Hills. The last mile or so was down a narrow country road and when we went round the final bend I could see, away to my right through the trees, white-flannelled figures about two meadows' distance. We turned right over a small bridge and drove into the tiny carpark behind a pavilion which looked like a small log cabin. John Waters, the son of the founder, greeted us and, as we came round the side of the pavilion, a small handkerchief of a ground opened in front of us. The home side was batting and there were eight or ten players between the two sides who had once worn the New Zealand cap; Ken Rutherford was a representative of the present side.

The Valley of Peace, Christchurch Cinema's Cricket Club, to give it its full name, was founded by Harry Waters in 1928. John Waters kindly gave me a booklet about the club which had been published many years ago. The description of the club and how it came to be founded is worth repeating in full.

Tucked away in the hills to the south of Christchurch, New Zealand, there is a valley that is well named 'The Valley of Peace'. You will not find it unless you have an efficient guide and there will be no guide for you unless you sincerely plan for a few hours to put aside the cares of business and of the world. When you come to it there will be above you a cloudless summer blue sky and you will rest your eyes on the green of a broad lawn and of lovely trees.

It is just a cricket ground, not a large one, beautifully kept and beautifully situated, which has been maintained for more than twenty years by the enthusiasm of a bare handful of men whose occupations bar them from organized games on any day but Sunday.

The idea of a cricket club for the staffs of theatres controlled by Christchurch Cinemas Ltd must have been born during some picnic game played on a bright Sunday afternoon. The difficulty was to find a playing area, because at that time the public parks and sportsgrounds were closed to Sunday play.

The solution was found by the kindness and interest of Miss White, then farming in the Hoon Hay Valley, who offered the use of a cow paddock of rather more than an acre, on condition that the cricketers themselves cleared the ground and put it in order. The first job was to remove old tree stumps and level the surface and the next was to scythe the long grass.

A close cut in the middle produced a wicket of sorts, and though the outfield was still very rough the enthusiasts were not daunted. As soon as might be they played their first match there. Other games followed, and as the players became more and more interested they began to think in new terms about the field and its surroundings. They were not going to be content with a wicket less than perfect, an outfield other than smooth, a game played otherwise than in strict accordance with the rules.

It was Miss White, who with her generosity made the next development possible, for she agreed to let the Club have the land on an indefinite lease at a rental of a shilling a week for each player to be paid to some charitable organization.

This briefly is how the Christchurch Cinema's Club came into existence. With the assistance of friends and supporters, equipment was purchased, water was brought onto the ground from a nearby creek, a pavilion built of rough logs, a refreshment room and a scoring box took form, the hedges were trimmed, the field was regularly mown and rolled and top dressed on occasion, until the Club had a ground which, if small, had a surface the equal of any in the city. All this was not accomplished without sweat and blistered hands. The labourers toiled unpaid, but they had the joy of seeing the ground take shape and they had the delight of a picnic lunch of grilled steak or sausages and chips, cooked in the open, or perhaps a cold boiled fowl contributed by a generous supporter.

The whole enterprise has been due in the main to the leadership of Mr Harry Waters, himself a cricketer of ability, who has never been content with anything short of the highest standard. Like Mrs Battle of pious memory, he demanded 'the rigour of the game'. The players had to be properly uniformed in whites, the matches had to be controlled by competent umpires and no deviation from the Laws of the game was to be tolerated. The field, as already indicated, was about an acre in extent. A boundary hit counts two, one over the boundary is four. If a ball in flight touches any part of a tree and is subsequently caught by a fieldsman the batsman is given not out.

Inevitably 'The Valley of Peace' has already found a place, though a modest one, in the literature of the game. In his book *For England and Yorkshire*, for instance, Herbert Sutcliffe speaks of the cricket grounds that come to his mind when he thinks of the trips he has made overseas. He goes on:

Then I think of the Newlands ground at Capetown in the most beautiful position, nestling at the foot of Table Mountain, and sometimes I think of that ground ten miles from Christchurch in New Zealand, the ground which is named 'The Valley of Peace' – a beautiful ground in the heart of the country, a ground on which no member of the fair sex is allowed. The name, as I have said, is 'The Valley of Peace'. On the back of the fixture card for 1934/35 of the Valley of Peace Cricket Club – the card arrived the other day – there is:
'Willow and Cane, nothing but that, oh but it's glorious, swinging the bat, leather and thread, there you have all – oh but it's glorious gripping the ball. Grass at our feet and the sun overhead, here let us play till the evening is red. Worries forgotten from care sweet surcease, oh but it's glorious, the Valley of Peace.'

And again on a later page Sutcliffe writes, 'I have told earlier of the Valley of Peace, the cricket ground on which men only are allowed to go, which is a few miles outside Christchurch. There I played for the local team and, with a not out hundred, qualified for a position on the honours board in that picturesque little pavilion with which this delightful ground is adorned.'

And here is a passage from *The Book of the Two Maurices* by Maurice Turnbull and Maurice Allom.

Nearly everyone on Sunday found his way to the Valley of Peace where the Christchurch Cinema's Cricket Club was being led against a visiting eleven by Mr Harry Waters, whose unassuming kindness became a household word among us. It was through his efforts that we were given the freedom of nearly all the cinemas in New Zealand. Lying in deckchairs on that pleasant ground, hidden deep away from the road by a surrounding belt of trees, nothing could break our peace: not the twittering of birds; not the sizzling of syphons; not the dull thud of bat meeting ball. 'Oh but it's glorious, the Valley of Peace.'

In its way there can be no finer acre of ground in the entire cricket world. The trees – oak, ash, elm, beech and poplar – combine with the hills to give it its character and the winding lane which leads there ensures its remoteness. The cricket is hard fought and the founder clearly felt that the rule forbidding ladies to the ground was appropriate for a spot which is named the Valley of Peace! Ladies have been allowed there once, in 1978, when they held a large party to celebrate the fiftieth anniversary of the club. They may not have their next chance until 2028. It is a rule which is taken seriously even today. While I was there, Jeremy Coney was expected to arrive. We heard a car draw up about 300 yards away, the door slammed and five minutes later Jeremy Coney, carrying two suitcases, walked onto the ground. When asked why he had walked the last few hundred yards he said that he had been given a lift by a lady and he knew that they were not welcome. It is a perfect spot and, when I left after lending a hand to wash up the lunch things, I felt as though I had been trapped for a few hours on an idyllic desert island. The glories of the Valley of Peace were underlined even more emphatically when I had to go straight to Napier and then on to Auckland to watch the last two one-day internationals between England and New Zealand. My heart remained very firmly in the Valley of Peace.

Then it was back to Australia, a fine wine dinner in Melbourne, two days on Hayman Island – the ultimate holiday island on the Great Barrier Reef – and on to Honolulu and the Sheraton Group's Royal Hawaiian Hotel in order to get to grips with the start of this book. Thanks to my old friends Peter and Marie Louisa Thompson – he is the general manager – I found myself in a delicious suite overlooking the bay. I only hope this book does justice to it and the Mai Tai bar.

After that it was the long flight back to England and the start of another English cricket season. The first fixture for me was Denis Compton's seventieth birthday party for 600 people at the Intercontinental Hotel at Hyde Park Corner. It was a glorious, unashamedly nostalgic occasion with Denis's cricketing friends and colleagues as well as legendary names from his days with Arsenal at Highbury. Tim Rice, who organized the raffle, mentioned in his speech that the first few four-day games had been a great advertisement for this form of the game. He listed some of the more notable achievements so far and went on to say that he was able to tell us that Ian Botham had claimed five successive victims, all of them in economy class. John Warr, President of the MCC, also spoke and began by saying, 'To be President of MCC you have to be in the springtime of your senility.' Colin Cowdrey talked of the birthday boy's cricket. He remembered batting with him for England at Melbourne in 1954–55. Keith Miller, who had flown across for the dinner, had bowled to Compton and the first ball pitched on the middle stump and missed the off. As Keith started his walk back he looked at Cowdrey at the non-striker's end and said, 'You know, Colin, I've been bowling him this rubbish for eight years, but he still doesn't get any better!'

Two days later I drove up the M1 to Northampton where I watched Dennis Lillee bowl his first overs for Northamptonshire. He may have lost some of his hair at the age of thirty-nine, and a little pace, but none of his skill. He took six for 68 in the second innings – but, hang on, if I'm not careful I shall be getting stuck into another cricket season already.

— 15 —

An Unpleasant Aftermath

1988 season: Gatting causes upsets with his book • tabloids go to
town on 'England captain's sex romp' • Gatting sacked •
deterioration of behavioural standards, particularly Chris Broad's •
selectors and players need a new approach.

But within a few short weeks events were unwinding at such a pace that it
was impossible not to be caught up in a new web. The season had begun
with the exploits of two well known individuals far away from the game of
cricket. 'The Galloping Major', Major Ronald Ferguson, had kept the
headline writers on the tabloids more than fully occupied until he was
overtaken by Frank Bough's antics. I daresay they both caused a good
deal of tutt-tutting in certain quarters, but all the world loves the salacious
details. Who could honestly say – not many I bet – that they were not keen
to hear and read more when the stories first broke? Mike Gatting
completed this particular hat-trick during the First Test Match in
Nottingham, making sure that the game of cricket and his name was on
everyone's lips. The overwhelming truth in all three of these episodes is
simply that if you are in the entertainment industry and you behave
exotically, you get your name in the papers. But we are getting way ahead
of the story.

We have looked at a number of England captains in these pages, and
maybe Gatting's was the most curious reign of all. As we have seen, he
could do nothing about the almost completed Indian series or the New
Zealanders who followed when he took over from David Gower in 1986.
He then managed to retain the Ashes in Australia, which is one the game's
hardest assignments. Imran Khan's Pakistanis were too strong in England
in 1987, and after that came the extraordinary winter of 1987–88. Gatting
took England to the World Cup Final in Calcutta and lost by seven runs to
Australia. Then he walked straight into the extraordinary machinations of
Mr Haseeb Ahsan in Pakistan, which grew altogether too much for
Gatting, his players and eventually the management too, who by the end
were coming out in a strong defence of the indefensible. Finally, after
behaviour which has known no parallel in modern Test history, the Test
and County Cricket Board made the extraordinary gift of one thousand
pounds to each player – a gift which deserved to rebound on the Board.

Two weeks in England over Christmas will have seen plenty of straight talking, and afterwards in Australia and New Zealand the manager, Peter Lush, emerged from his corner to smack Broad and Dilley over the wrists with fines for bad behaviour which some may have felt hardly fitted the crime. In New Zealand, England continued to remonstrate with the umpires and to show dissent, but not at Pakistani levels, and indeed returned home with missives from their hosts talking of their excellent behaviour – missives which hardly backed up impressions gained by those who actually saw events in New Zealand.

By the time the 1988 season began the England players could not surely have been in any doubt as to the behavioural standards they had to maintain. The West Indies were beaten in all three one-day internationals for the Texaco Trophy and the circus moved to Trent Bridge for the First Test Match. The initial sound of gunfire, after England's collapse on the opening day, came with news that Gatting's soon-to-be-published book contained a chapter telling his own story about events in Pakistan. One heard that he had originally written the book himself and, as the terms of his contract with the TCCB states, had shown it to the authorities at Lord's. Not surprisingly, at a time when they were trying to rebuild bridges with Pakistan, they threw it back at him and told him that the chapter about events over there when he shook his finger at umpire Shakoor Rana were not permissible. The manuscript reappeared again as the work of a lady journalist, and Gatting's thoughts and reports from Pakistan were told in the third person. The TCCB did not fall for that one either. The chief executive, Alan Smith, said during the Trent Bridge Test, having read the offending chapter, that if it appeared in its present form it would not do Gatting's chances of retaining the captaincy any good. (He had only been appointed for the first two Test Matches of the series.)

It was not the least extraordinary aspect of this unbelievable saga. Gatting had behaved in a shameful manner when he took on umpire Shakoor Rana in mid-pitch in Faisalabad. The fact that the provocation was extreme was no excuse and he was extremely lucky to get away with it – if those in charge of the side had been able to distance themselves further from events they would have seen it all for what it was, and I doubt he would have been appointed at the start of the West Indies series in England. Indeed he might even have been replaced for the New Zealand leg of the tour which followed after Christmas. It was nothing short of madness, therefore, for Gatting to have deliberately precipitated a confrontation with the Test and County Cricket Board over his book. The whole incident revealed an astonishing lack of sensitivity by a chap who has never been over-blessed with imagination. It showed, too, that while he may be the bravest cricketer of the lot, he is not perhaps the brightest. The entire episode told of his obstinacy, his determination to prove himself right at all costs, even to the extent of losing the captaincy, which I cannot believe he would not have foreseen as a probable consequence. When Gatting returned to England for that Christmas break he said that he expected to be dumped from the captaincy. Maybe he had a death-wish. In everyone's interest, and most of all his own, the subject of Pakistan needed to be left well alone.

If Gatting's, or to be more exact the lady who put his words onto paper, literary efforts put a cloud over the latter part of the First Test Match, it was merely a haze over the sun compared to the cyclone which lay just around the corner. The match ended on the Tuesday in a draw, the first time England had escaped defeat in eleven Test Matches against the West Indies, which was a matter certainly not to be ignored. On the Wednesday morning we all woke to headlines in some sectors of the tabloid press claiming that England players had been involved in a late-night sex romp in the team hotel, which was situated mid-way between Nottingham and Leicester. The following day Gatting was named as the principal offender and a lusty, busty waitress from a neighbouring restaurant, which the England players frequented, told all. According to press reports she had been taken to Gatting's room and bonked, roughly but not kinkily. All hell broke loose, not surprisingly.

There were so many points at issue, but the saddest part of it all was that the game of cricket had once again been let down resoundingly by those who should have known better. While there is no reason to doubt Gatting's version of the story, muck-raking journalism is not a new feature of life and high-profile sportsmen have been as aware of it as anyone for sometime now. On the cricket front anyone who has played for England in the last five or six years must have been all too conscious of it in view of the incidents in which Ian Botham had been supposedly involved and of the press reaction to each one of them. On the face of it, why should it be the concern of anyone, except the man involved and his wife maybe, if he does meet an attractive girl who is available and willing and the inevitable happens? It has been happening to travelling sportsmen ever since sport was invented and it is not for the Test selectors or tabloid newspapers to sit in judgement on the morals of that. One duty of the authorities, however, is to look after and protect the game of cricket and to make sure if at all possible that it does not fall into disrepute. Tabloid newspapers are only interested in their circulation.

The cricket world was now in a state of turmoil and, while newspapers were busily collecting sworn affidavits from ladies who were said to be involved, the cricket authorities were also burning up the telephone wires. The cricket manager, Micky Stewart, had travelled down to Swansea on the Tuesday night to watch the Benson and Hedges semi-final between Glamorgan and Derbyshire. When the news broke in the Wednesday newspapers he spent a very different day from the one he intended. One gathered that he talked to as many of the England players as he was able to get hold of by telephone. Then came the announcement that the four players who he had been unable to reach had been called to Lord's on the Friday. It was an astonishingly insensitive action by the TCCB, for they failed at the same time to say that it was part of a routine investigation and that they were not in any way suggesting that the four were guilty of bad behaviour. As it was, the world thought that the finger was being pointed as these four, although they were all exonerated and as far as I know there was not the slightest suspicion that any of them had been involved. Another problem was that the original story had spoken about heaving bottoms in long grass on the Leicestershire/ Nottinghamshire borders. Who did they belong to? I daresay many people wanted to know the answer to that one.

The four players came to Lord's and on his departure from the pavilion one of them, Allan Lamb, pulled down the window of his taxi and gave the assembled press an impressive broadside. On his return home to Northamptonshire he apparently got together with his solicitors and started to issue solicitors' letters like confetti. I should know because the BBC received one after my own efforts on the *One O'Clock News* on the Friday afternoon. I had said, when asked, that I had expected the four would drive to Lord's and 'get away with it', which of course implies guilt – the last thing I meant. However Lamb sprang into action in my and other directions although I doubt he will get very fat from what he collects. Anyway, I hope that reputations were not harmed when the sound of gunfire had faded away.

Later in the week Gatting was interviewed by the TCCB at Lord's, and afterwards Peter May read out a statement in the press box and Micky Stewart answered the questions which came afterwards. Stewart was in a difficult position. For some time now, in answer to press questioning, he had been making plausible excuses for poor England cricket and even worse behaviour. Yet all that had happened to damage the image of England's cricket in the last few months had been under his managership. After the marvellous start he had made in Australia, he too had become much too close to the players. He was a part of the same club. A captain, a cricket manager and an overall manager will have, by the nature of their jobs, to take an unpopular line from time to time. It is essential therefore that they are able to distance themselves from the rest of the side. If those in authority are, in effect, no more than three of the boys, objectivity disappears and independent action with it. This difficult time has underlined some important lessons.

May's statement to the press that day at Lord's read as follows:

'Following a meeting of the selectors at Lord's today, the chairman, Peter May, said that the invitation to Mike Gatting to captain the England team in the Second Cornhill Test Match at Lord's starting on 16 June had been withdrawn.

'Gatting had been seen by the selectors earlier in the day and he had informed them that allegations of sexual misconduct by him which had appeared in the national press were without any foundation and were strongly denied. His solicitors would be serving writs alleging libel against the newspapers concerned.

'The selectors emphasized that they did not believe the allegations in the newspapers and accepted Gatting's account of what happened. May said, however, that the selectors were concerned that Gatting had behaved irresponsibly during a Test Match by inviting female company to his room for a drink in the late evening. Warnings had previously been issued to all England players concerning the standard of behaviour expected of them at all times both on and off the field and these had been ignored.

'The selection of the England team will be postponed until tomorrow when a new captain for the Lord's Test will be appointed. In all the circumstances Gatting has informed the selectors he does not wish to be considered for selection for this particular match.

'The England team manager, Micky Stewart, has been making enquiries about "alleged" events involving other England players and these are continuing. It was anticipated that the enquiries would be completed tomorrow morning before the selectors pick the England team later in the day.'

It was ostensibly the product of muddled thinking. If taken at face value Gatting was sacked because he had the temerity to take a girl to his room for a birthday drink late one evening during a Test Match. We were told that nothing else was taken into account by the selectors and that they entirely believed Gatting's version of the story when he said most emphatically that he did not make love to the girl. Fair enough. But if Gatting had not gone to Pakistan and had not therefore written that chapter in his book, would he have lost the captaincy for taking a girl to his room for a late night drink during a Test match? I pose the question.

In the immediate aftermath when a number of those involved were understandably under considerable pressure, I even heard it said that it was a put-up job by a newspaper – difficult to say which one for so many had the story – and that the girl concerned had been promised in advance a five figure sum and a free holiday in America for her pains. I was told this by someone not a million miles from the centre of it all, although not a member of the team, and I can only say that it will have suited some people to think that this was true.

The hounding of innocents by newspapers is intolerable and in these incidents the truth almost invariably lies somewhere between the extremes one hears expressed. The undeniable truth seems to be that all the world loves a gossip and a good scandal. A headline reading 'England Captain Involved In Sex Romp During First Test' is almost impossible to resist. Gatting would have known only too well the ways of the popular press, for he also was only too well aware of what had happened to Ian Botham over the years. As captain of his country, though, he had a responsibility which goes beyond that of any others in his side. He must be seen, like Caesar's wife, to be above suspicion. As England's captain he should have been conscious of this at all times and should not have put himself into a potentially compromising situation. The cricketers may say that this has always gone on; probably it has, but in the old days the focus of the media was not so sharp and players' private lives were not so ruthlessly pursued. It is worth modern players remembering that they are now being paid good money, which is far in excess of anything their predecessors took home. More money brings with it the need for a greater sense of responsibility.

In the end the England selectors had no alternative but to sack Gatting in order to protect the game of cricket. The whole story shows that his judgement was poor, and in any event he had not been a particularly good captain, having gone for a string of fourteen matches without a victory. He was, too, very lucky to have survived the Pakistan affair when it seemed to me that he forfeited all right to continue as England's captain. The selectors will not have enjoyed making the decision but they must have made the right one. In a sense Gatting was unlucky, just as he had been in Pakistan. Bad luck is at best a dubious defence, and maybe it is something which those in responsible positions should guard against.

When Micky Stewart, Gatting and Peter Lush joined forces to take England to Australia in 1986–87 it was a new beginning. A disastrous start to that tour was overcome, as we have seen, and the Ashes series and the two one-day competitions were all won. All responsible critics will have felt the need to be cautious in their praise, not least because of the standard of Australian cricket. The principal participants will have been more delighted than anyone. Stewart returned home to find a three-year contract waiting for him as permanent England cricket manager and Gatting will have felt that he had cracked it. Over-confidence can be dangerous.

Not surprisingly, perhaps, a touch of arrogance crept in which was not affected by Pakistan's victory in 1987, although they were clearly the better side. It was a triumph to reach the World Cup Final later in the year and not such a set-back to lose the final by such a narrow margin to Australia. The party will have gone to Pakistan after the final without any thought of what was lying in wait for them. Lush was again the overall manager as a reward for doing the job so well in Australia, and indeed he has been appointed permanent Overseas Manager, while Stewart and Gatting had all the confidence of a reasonably successful double act. Lush had become an affable if slightly pompous figurehead, Stewart, a master at avoiding the direct question and adept at dealing in platitudes whenever necessary, while Gatting himself had become extremely self-assured.

When Haseeb Ahsan's plans, which seemed curious to say the least, became clear during the First Test Match in Lahore, surprise turned rapidly to shock horror, to be swiftly followed by preposterous indignation.

I have written earlier how teams are thrown together more on tours of India and Pakistan because there are fewer alternatives to the team room in the evenings than there are in other countries. It was now and because of this that the three in charge made the mistake of not keeping their distance from the rest of the side. If you are one of the boys, as I have said, it is almost impossible to be a disciplinarian too. Broad refused to walk in Lahore and, we are told, received a reprimand. Of course, the provocation built up alarmingly, but when Gatting had his confrontation with Shakoor Rana it appeared to be with the support of the management, at least it was not followed by a ringing condemnation. Gatting was then ordered to apologise by Lord's and Lush and Stewart formed squares with the team. Discipline had broken down. There were clearly faults on both sides and yet by remaining so close to the players the English management were never able to take an objective view-point and to see that both sides had made mistakes. Raman Subba Row and Alan Smith of the Test and County Cricket Board flew out from Lord's insisting that Gatting apologise to umpire Shakoor Rana, which he did most reluctantly. The two itinerant officials probably found a sense of outrage in the party which will have surprised them, and they will have had to have argued against the management as well as the players. The result of this was the strange decision by Subba Row to give every member of the tour a bonus of a thousand pounds on their return.

And so to the start on the 1988 season in England, and I use the phrase advisedly when I write that those in authority on that tour had got away with it. England made a splendid start against the West Indies, winning all three one-day games and then drawing the first Test at Trent Bridge. By then, Gatting's obstinate arrogance – for that was surely what it was – had been seen again in his determination to publish his version of the Shakoor Rana incident and be damned. Maybe he felt he could not be touched. Maybe it was with iron in his soul that he encountered the aforementioned busty waitress at the team's hotel or in the restaurant they were visiting. He may have thought he could get away with anything; my own feeling is that he gave it no thought at all. When it all became public news he paid the penalty. By a strange irony it was announced two days later that the new secretary of the Pakistan Board of Control had said that Shakoor Rana would never stand in another Test Match. Maybe one good turn deserved another.

Gatting's apparent death-wish became all the more apparent as the summer progressed. Quite reasonably, in the immediate aftermath of being sacked, he asked not to be considered for the Second Test at Lord's.

He was brought back as a player for the Third Test and failed in both innings. It was then that he again asked not to be considered, for he said that he was not in the right frame of mind, and was not therefore chosen for the Fourth Test. When that match was over he announced that he was not available for the winter's tour of India. After all that he had done surely his duty should have been to answer every call the selectors made upon him – and to be extremely grateful for each call that was made. I felt that by opting out now he showed how unfit he was ever to have been made captain of England.

It was, to say the least, a meaningful irony that on the Tuesday before the Fifth Test Match against the West Indies at the Oval, Gatting and his family should have gone to Buckingham Palace, and that he should have been invested with the OBE for services rendered to cricket. The very next day he was fined £5000 by the Test and County Cricket Board for the 'ghosted' chapter in his autobiography about the goings on in Pakistan, with the caution that if it had not been for his record the fine would have been doubled. The day after that he had the gall to appear on the England balcony on the first day of the Fifth Test. Services to cricket indeed. . . .

I suppose it is old fashioned to believe that the phrase 'it isn't cricket' with all its meanings is still important. If so, I can only admit that my state of middle age is more advanced than I thought. Cricket is such a wonderful game and very much because of the principles, the behaviour, the deportment which have marched in step with it since those dim distant days when it was first played. It has always had something to do with all that is decent in life. Earlier in the book I have taken the Cardus point that cricket is at any one time a reflection of the society that nurtures it; that must go for behavioural standards too.

While Gatting and one or two non-cricket playing celebrities got up to their pranks in 1988, which in Gatting's case cannot have done any good to the game, a gentleman called Chris Broad was doing his best to buck the inherent decencies of cricket and was repeatedly behaving as though he considered himself to be above all that. We have seen Broad, a highly competent opening batsman, discard Gloucestershire and move to his 'more fashionable' Nottinghamshire. We have also seen him stand forever in his crease when given out in a Test Match in Pakistan until his partner, Graham Gooch, had to come down the pitch and tell him to be on his way. Few things have gone more against the spirit of the game of cricket and what it stands for than that payment of one thousand pounds per man to the England side in Pakistan for bad behaviour. And yet was that arbitrary decision ever questioned by the county representatives? We also saw Broad in a temper knock his stumps over when dismissed in the Bicentennial Test in Sydney, and now we have seen him mouth obscenities when given out in the Second Test against the West Indies at Lord's in 1988, and he has always been reluctant to admit that he was out when the umpire's finger has risen against him. To round-off this sorry saga he has now been named the chief culprit in the dressing room in-fighting at Trent Bridge which has done so much to undermine the captaincy of Tim Robinson, who succeeded Clive Rice in 1988. It is a squalid record. To their great credit Nottinghamshire told the world what had happened and pointed a finger at Broad, so that no one could be in any doubt as to where the fault lay. How much better and more honourable it would have been if those in charge of England's cricket over this period had faced up to his actions rather than issued another catalogue of lame excuses which cheapened both them and the game of cricket. The cricket manager, originally appointed after the disastrous West Indies series in the West Indies on a disciplinary ticket, has not come out of any of this too well for so much of it has happened under his jurisdiction. One is left to wonder what he has been doing.

In one of the more extraordinary incidents in 1988, which on its own did the image of cricket nothing but harm, the selectors apparently disagreed among themselves when picking the squad of players for the Third Test Match against the West Indies at Old Trafford. At Lord's, when given out, Broad had again shown obvious dissent, obvious to all but England's cricket manager, who afterwards walked down the well-worn path of hoping to avoid the issue by talking of disappointment rather than dissent. The press made much of the subsequent selectorial disagreement and it seemed to be that Peter May, the chairman, was keen to drop Broad while the other selectors, including the new captain, John Emburey, wanted to keep him. The majority won. Yet I cannot believe that any of the others – Stewart, Titmus and Sharpe as well as Emburey – would, while playing, ever have behaved as Broad had done. They appeared by picking Broad to be defending the indefensible.

The behaviour by Test cricketers on and off the field in the period this book covers has considerably deteriorated. As it has happened the nerve of the authorities who control these things appears to have gone, or at any rate they have become much more tolerant of unacceptable behaviour. I wonder if they realize how badly they have let down the game. I wonder too, if you look at the top echelons of cricket administrators, whether those concerned are not so caught up in their own search for power and the need to guard their backs that they forget that their main responsibility is to the game of cricket and not to themselves. Could it be that in offices at Lord's and elsewhere people are being leap-frogged over one another or being moved sideways so that the throne is not threatened? Those whom it concerns must realize too that continual bad performances by England do not, to say the least, reflect well on those in charge and therefore comes the need for smoke-screens, excuses and anything that prevents reality from hitting home and the truth from being revealed.

Let us go back to the aftermath of the Gatting affair. John Emburey, an affable, avuncular off-spinner from Lord's, who has sadly forgotten how to take wickets anymore, was appointed as a caretaker captain. The next two Test Matches were lost and, worse still for him, he bowled both reluctantly and unsuccessfully. Those in charge decided he had to go and then embarked upon another farce which made the public, that nebulous body who pays the bills and yet is so seldom considered, regard those who run the game as something approaching figures of fun. We were promised an announcement from Lord's naming the new England captain on a Monday. It was put off until the Tuesday. Rumours raced around that the choice was Graham Gooch, the man who had resigned the Essex captaincy the year before because of a significant lack of success and the effect it had on his own batting form. There was a hiccup: Gooch had said he would not tour again and there was no point in turning to him if he was not prepared to take the side to India in 1988–89. An uneasy silence from Lord's; had Gooch been approached? Some said yes, some said no. Another day of indecision. The announcement was now to be made on Wednesday. Apparently Gooch said he had not been approached, then rumour had it that an indirect approach had been made to him, whatever that may have meant, and there followed another stuttering announcement that a decision would not now come until the Thursday. Indecision had been turned into an art form.

What were we all to think? Much more, what were the public to think? It had become a farce. On the Thursday a little bit of sanity returned and Chris Cowdrey was appointed. Critics then immediately said things about Peter May appointing his godson, as though it was the ultimate in nepotism, which was a monstrous charge for May would only have appointed Cowdrey for the reason that he thought he was the best man for the job. As Cowdrey was his godson, May will have appointed him in spite of that and not because of it. I have been critical of May in these pages but most certainly not on this count.

Some of us were left with the thought that those who make these choices were frantically trying to hang on to as many of the old lot, who had become well tried and trusted failures, for as long they could. Maybe they felt it was easier to have a captain who had been in the side for sometime and where everyone knew how to get along together. Maybe it felt more comfortable that way. It was obvious to any outsider that a new start was needed. The old lot, if they had been called up for the Fourth Test at Headingley, would have dumped their bags in the familiar corners of the dressing room, changed, shrugged their shoulders and gloomily have got ready to face another defeat. What was needed was fresh-faced enthusiasm from new players with a point to prove and a desire to make good their places in the England side. In the end that was almost what we got. Cowdrey, the captain, Tim Curtis, Robin Smith, but why no Kim Barnett and Jack Russell I don't know. I just hope it all signals the beginning of a new approach by England on the field and a shake-up in the corridors of power, for I believe this is needed as urgently as a shake-up in the dressing room. The West Indies will continue to beat England for the foreseeable future – and did so most convincingly at Headingley – and I doubt anything will change that but it is the manner of the defeat rather than the defeat itself which is so crucially important. We have had make-do-and-mend and muddled compromise for far too long – almost to the point where it seemed to have become a mutual protection racket. The authorities have in recent years fallen over backwards to accommodate Ian Botham and his antics; I think one can see from all that has gone before in these pages that they have set a dangerous precedent.

As a penultimate and most unsatisfactory postscript, the selectors, in their infinite wisdom, brought back Philip DeFreitas when injury caused Graham Dilley to drop out of the side for the Fifth Test at the Oval. DeFreitas had been dropped after the Third Test and on returning to play for Leicestershire had to be disciplined by his county for not trying in their game against Derbyshire. DeFreitas had the gall to say that he was piqued at being left out of the England side for the Fourth Test. Leicestershire's reaction was splendid, as one would expect from a club run by Mike Turner, and yet he was immediately let down comprehensively by the England selectors who delivered DeFreitas back into the Test side at the first opportunity. I believe the time has long since come – and I write these words on the eve of the Fifth Test against the West Indies – when the only honourable course of action left for the selectors is to resign *en bloc* before they do any more harm, not only to England's cricket, but, most important of all, to everything the game of cricket stands for. This last is a fearful indictment but one I believe they deserve. By the time these words are read I wonder just who of all the characters I have mentioned will be negotiating with South Africa.

This final paragraph comes after the last Test against the West Indies. Chris Cowdrey and Kim Barnett, selected at last, could not play because of injuries and Gooch captained the side while Robert Bailey and Matthew Maynard got their chance. The spirit was excellent, Neil Foster bowled magnificently, England gained a small first innings lead but went on to lose by eight wickets. At the end of it all, I came away certain that England's cricket had a future, but it was in spite rather than because of those that run the game and select the sides. At last we had a thrilling, red-blooded contest and after it I only wait in fear and trepidation to see the line-up the selectors announce for the 1988–89 tour of India. There comes a time when the only honourable course is to fall on your sword.

Statistics

Australia *v* West Indies 1984–85:

FIRST TEST MATCH (Perth), 9–12 November. *West Indies* 416 (Gomes 127, Dujon 139). *Australia* 76 (Holding 6/21) and 228 (Wood 56; Marshall 4/68). West Indies won by an innings and 112 runs.

SECOND TEST MATCH (Brisbane), 23–26 November. *Australia* 175 (Garner 4/67) and 271 (Wessels 61; Marshall 5/82). *West Indies* 424 (Richardson 138, Lloyd 114) and 26 for 2 wickets. West Indies won by eight wickets.

THIRD TEST MATCH (Adelaide), 7–11 December. *West Indies* 356 (Greenidge 95, Lloyd 78; Lawson 8/112) and 292 for 7 wickets declared (Gomes 120 not out). *Australia* 284 (Wessels 98; Marshall 5/69) and 173 (Wessels 70; Marshall 5/38). West Indies won by 191 runs.

FOURTH TEST MATCH (Melbourne), 22–27 December. *West Indies* 479 (Richards 208) and 186 for 5 wickets declared. *Australia* 296 (Wessels 90; Marshall 5/86) and 198 for 8 wickets (Hilditch 113). Match drawn.

FIFTH TEST MATCH (Sydney), 30,31 December, 1,2 January. *Australia* 471 for 9 wickets declared (Wessels 173). *West Indies* 163 (Holland 6/54) and 253 (Lloyd 72; Holland 4/90). Australia won by an innings and 55 runs.

West Indies *v* England 1985–86:

FIRST TEST MATCH (Kingston, Jamaica), 21–23 February. *England* 159 (Patterson 4/30) and 152 (Willey 71; Garner 3/22, Marshall 3/29). *West Indies* 307 (Ellison 5/78) and 5 for no wicket. West Indies won by ten wickets.

SECOND TEST MATCH (Port of Spain, Trinidad), 7–12 March. *England* 176 (Gower 66; Marshall 4/38) and 315 (extras 59). *West Indies* 399 (Richardson 102; Emburey 5/78) and 95 for 3 wickets. West Indies won by seven wickets.

THIRD TEST MATCH (Bridgetown, Barbados), 21–25 March. *West Indies*

418 (Richardson 160). *England* 189 (Gower 66; Marshall 4/42) and 199 (Garner 4/69, Patterson 3/28). West Indies won by an innings and 30 runs.

FOURTH TEST MATCH (Port of Spain, Trinidad), 3–5 April. *England* 200 (Garner 4/43) and 150 (Garner 3/15). *West Indies* 312 (Botham 5/71) and 39 for no wicket. West Indies won by ten wickets.

FIFTH TEST MATCH (St John's, Antigua), 11–16 April. *West Indies* 474 (Haynes 131) and 246 for 2 wickets declared (Richards 110 not out). *England* 310 (Gower 90; Garner 4/67) and 170 (Gooch 51; Harper 3/10). West Indies won by 240 runs.

England *v* India 1986:

FIRST CORNHILL TEST MATCH (Lord's), 5–10 June. *England* 294 (Gooch 114; Sharma 5/64) and 180 (Kapil Dev 4/52, Maninder 3/9). *India* 341 (Vengsarkar 126 not out) and 136 for 5 wickets. India won by five wickets.

SECOND CORNHILL TEST MATCH (Leeds), 19–23 June. *India* 272 (Vengsarkar 61) and 237 (Vengsarkar 102 not out). *England* 102 (Binny 5/40, Madan Lal 3/18) and 128 (Maninder 4/26). India won by 279 runs.

THIRD CORNHILL TEST MATCH (Birmingham), 3–8 July. *England* 390 (Gatting 183 not out) and 235 (Sharma 6/58). *India* 390 and 174 for 5 wickets (Edmonds 4/31). Match drawn.

England *v* New Zealand 1986:

FIRST CORNHILL TEST MATCH (Lord's), 24–29 July. *England* 307 (Moxon 74; Hadlee 6/80) and 295 for 6 wickets declared (Gooch 183). *New Zealand* 342 (M.D. Crowe 106; Dilley 4/82, Edmonds 4/97) and 41 for 2 wickets. Match drawn.

SECOND CORNHILL TEST MATCH (Nottingham), 7–12 August. *England* 256 (Gower 71; Hadlee 6/80) and 230 (Emburey 75; Hadlee 4/60). *New Zealand* 413 (Bracewell 110) and 77 for 2 wickets. New Zealand won by eight wickets.

THIRD CORNHILL TEST MATCH (Oval), 21–26 August. *New Zealand* 287

(Wright 119; Dilley 4/92) and 7 for no wicket. *England* 388 for 5 wickets declared (Gower 131, Gatting 121). Match drawn.

Australia *v* England 1986–87:

FIRST TEST MATCH (Brisbane), 14–19 November. *England* 456 (Botham 138) and 77 for 3 wickets. *Australia* 248 (Dilley 5/68) and 282 (Marsh 110; Emburey 5/80). England won by seven wickets.

SECOND TEST MATCH (Perth), 28–30 November, 2,3 December. *England* 592 for 8 wickets declared (Broad 162, Gower 136, Richards 133) and 199 for 8 wickets declared. *Australia* 401 (Border 125; Dilley 4/79) and 197 for 4 wickets. Match drawn.

THIRD TEST MATCH (Adelaide), 12–16 December. *Australia* 514 for 5 wickets declared (Boon 103) and 201 for 3 wickets declared (Border 100 not out). *England* 455 (Broad 116, Gatting 100; Reid 4/64) and 39 for 2 wickets. Match drawn.

FOURTH TEST MATCH (Melbourne), 26–28 December. *Australia* 141 (Botham 5/41, Small 5/48) and 194 (Edmonds 3/45, Emburey 2/43). *England* 349 (Broad 112; Reid 4/78, McDermott 4/83). England won by an innings and 14 runs.

FIFTH TEST MATCH (Sydney), 10–15 January. *Australia* 343 (Jones 184 not out; Small 5/75) and 251 (Emburey 7/78). *England* 275 (Gower 72; Taylor 6/78) and 264 (Gatting 96; Sleep 5/72). Australia won by 55 runs.

New Zealand *v* West Indies 1987:

FIRST TEST MATCH (Wellington), 20–24 February. *New Zealand* 228 (Garner 5/51) and 386 for 5 wickets declared (Wright 138, M.D. Crowe 119). *West Indies* 345 (Haynes 121) and 50 for 2 wickets. Match drawn.

SECOND TEST MATCH (Auckland), 1–3 March. *West Indies* 418 for 9 wickets declared (Greenidge 213) and 16 for no wicket. *New Zealand* 157 (Marshall 4/43) and 273 (M.D. Crowe 104; Walsh 5/73). West Indies won by ten wickets.

THIRD TEST MATCH (Christchurch), 12–15 March. *West Indies* 100 (Hadlee 6/50) and 264 (Snedden 5/68). *New Zealand* 332 for 9 wickets declared (M.D. Crowe 83) and 33 for 5 wickets. New Zealand won by five wickets.

Reliance World Cup Final (50 overs):

AUSTRALIA *v* ENGLAND. Calcutta, 8 November. *Australia* 253 for 5 wickets (Boon 75). *England* 246 for 8 wickets (Athey 58). Australia won by seven runs. Man of the Match: D.C.Boon.

Australia *v* New Zealand 1987:

FIRST TEST MATCH (Brisbane), 4–7 December. *New Zealand* 186 (M.D. Crowe 67) and 212 (Patel 62). *Australia* 305 (Boon 143) and 97 for 1 wicket. Australia won by nine wickets.

SECOND TEST MATCH (Adelaide), 11–15 December. *New Zealand* 485 for 9 wickets declared (Jones 150, M.D.Crowe 137) and 182 for 7 wickets (Jones 64). *Australia* 496 (Border 205; Hadlee 5/68). Match drawn.

THIRD TEST MATCH (Melbourne), 26–30 December. *New Zealand* 317 (Wright 99, M.D. Crowe 82; McDermott 5/97) and 286 (M.D. Crowe 79; Dodemaide 6/58). *Australia* 357 (Sleep 90; Hadlee 5/109) and 230 for 9 wickets (Hadlee 5/67). Match drawn.

Bicentennial Test Match 1988:

AUSTRALIA *v* ENGLAND. Sydney, 29–31 January, 1,2 February. *England* 425 (Broad 139; Taylor 4/84). *Australia* 214 and 328 for 2 wickets (Boon 184 not out). Match drawn.

New Zealand *v* England 1988:

FIRST TEST MATCH (Christchurch), 12–17 February. *England* 319 (Broad 114, Robinson 70; Morrison 5/69) and 152 (Chatfield 4/36). *New Zealand* 168 (Dilley 6/38) and 130 for 4 wickets. Match drawn.

SECOND TEST MATCH (Auckland), 25–29 February. *New Zealand* 301 (Wright 103; Dilley 5/60) and 350 for 7 wickets declared (Greatbatch 107 not out). *England* 323 (Moxon 99; Chatfield 4/37). Match drawn.

THIRD TEST (Wellington), 3–7 March. *New Zealand* 512 for 6 wickets declared (M.D. Crowe 143, Rutherford 107). *England* 183 for 2 wickets (Moxon 81 not out, Broad 61). Match drawn.

Index